UND...
YOUR OWN
POWER

Other Books by the Authors

Freeing Someone You Love from Alcohol and Other Drugs

Relapse Traps: How to Avoid the 12 Most Common Pitfalls in Recovery

If It Runs in Your Family: Reducing the Risk of Alcoholism

Don't Help: A Positive Guide to Working with the Alcoholic

The Twelve Steps Revisited

The Healing Bond: Treating Addictions in Groups

UNDER YOUR OWN POWER

A Secular Approach to Twelve Step Programs

Ronald L. Rogers
and
Chandler Scott McMillin

A Perigee Book
Developed by The Philip Lief Group, Inc.

Perigee Books
are published by
The Putnam Publishing Group
200 Madison Avenue
New York, NY 10016

First Perigee Edition 1993

Library of Congress Cataloging-in-Publication Data

Rogers, Ronald.
Under your own power : a secular approach to Twelve Step
programs / Ronald L. Rogers and Chandler Scott McMillin.—
1st Perigee ed.
p.   cm.
"Developed by The Philip Lief Group, Inc."
Includes index.
ISBN 0-399-51849-5 (alk. paper)
1. Alcoholics—Rehabilitation.   2. Narcotics addicts—
Rehabilitation.   3. Agnostics—Mental health.   4. Atheists—Mental
health.   5. Twelve-step programs.   6. Self-help techniques.
I. McMillin, Chandler.   II. Philip Lief Group.   III. Title.
RC565.R567   1993   93-4803 CIP
616.86'0651—dc20

Cover design by Judith Kazdym Leeds

Printed in the United States of America
1 2 3 4 5 6 7 8 9 10

This book is printed on acid-free paper.
∞

Acknowledgments

WE WOULD LIKE to thank Gene Brissie and Laura Shepherd of Putnam; Philip Lief, Lee Ann Chearneyi, and The Philip Lief Group; and our agent and friend Bob Markel for helping to bring this book into existence.

We would also like to acknowledge the contribution of hundreds of skilled and creative clinicians whose work has contributed mightily to the philosophy and approach of the Chronic Disease Model. We may not have space to mention your name, but you have made a difference.

Contents

Chapter One

INTRODUCTION: RECOVERY FOR THE NONBELIEVER

WE ENTERED THE FLEDGLING FIELD of addictions treatment some twenty years ago, having been taught (as was nearly everyone else during that era) that alcoholics and drug addicts were psychologically disturbed individuals who could not stop drinking or taking drugs without extended, anxiety-provoking, even painful psychotherapy. After a few years working with recovering people, we realized this could not possibly be the case. The overwhelming majority of treatment successes did not graduate from the recommended course of therapy. In fact, most had never been in therapy at all—or if they had, quickly dropped out.

Paradoxically, many chronic failures—the patients who showed up in detox wards over and over, drunk, broken in spirit, miserable—were mired in exactly the kind of psychiatric care that we had been taught would cure them.

Frankly, we were stunned. It gradually dawned on us that what went on in psychiatric hospitals under the guise of treatment was, in fact, unwittingly teaching alcoholics and addicts how to *fail* at the difficult but relatively straightforward task of sobriety.

That was only one of many revelations. We discovered that the alcoholics our physicians blithely assured us were ready for discharge after three days of detoxification were, in fact, still experiencing exactly the kind of inner tremors, anxiety, and sleeplessness that would drive them back to drink as soon as they got home. We saw that, in contrast to their reputation for immaturity, many alcoholics were, in fact, capable of demonstrating exceptional judgment and responsibility, once away from alcohol. We learned that the tranquilizers given to alcoholics as they left the hospital, to help them "cope" with reality, instead made relapse virtually inevitable.

Most remarkably, we saw what the research literature said we would not find: widespread success. Alcoholics long since branded as hopeless by the institutions treating them often turned their lives around, to the amazement of their own counselors.

By the end of our fourth year in addictions, nearly every fondly held belief and academic doctrine from our college years had been destroyed by the greatest teacher of all—experience. And one of the most dramatic changes came in our understanding of the role of spirituality in recovery.

THE MYTH OF AA AS A RELIGIOUS ORGANIZATION

We began attending meetings of Alcoholics Anonymous soon after we entered the field. It wasn't entirely voluntary; as junior members of the staff, we were required by our superiors to accompany our patients to meetings, to protect them from who knew what (probably sobriety). Our preconception of AA came from the university psychologists who trained us: a quasi-religious organization irrelevant to the majority of alcoholics but of service to those few whose dependent personalities made them want to surrender their lives to the control of others. Though they would have denied it, our instructors considered sobriety in AA to be a sign of weakness instead of strength. "It's okay for some people," one informed us haughtily. "People who are uneducated."

What we found through our attendance at meetings was exactly the opposite. Far from a haven for the devout, Alcoholics Anonymous included many of the most skeptical individuals we had ever met. There was absolutely nothing slavish about their attitudes. They challenged every statement which wasn't directly obvious, and contended heatedly amongst themselves over the right and wrong response to situations other people would have taken for granted. We got used to hearing the phrase, "Hello, my name is Mary Ellen B., and I'm an alcoholic, and I think you're full of . . ."

So what was going on here?

After numerous attempts, we finally located an AA member who explained it to us satisfactorily. "You have to stop thinking of AA as a religion," he said. "It's more like the chamber of commerce. People come out of self-interest and stay because it is mutually beneficial. Also, it's cheap."

Another member, with twenty years sobriety, expanded on the relationship between the spiritual orientation of Alcoholics Anonymous and that of a church. "I see AA as the antithesis of organized religion," she explained. "Most of the people here bombed out of the churches they were raised in. They left because they don't like ritual, they don't like rules, they don't like being told what to do. A lot of them come to meetings because they think it helps them stay sober. Some of them come because they like the company of other drunks. A few of them probably come because they want to live a more spiritual life. And there are people who come just because they've been eighty-sixed [tossed out of] everywhere else. They figure we won't throw them out no matter how bad they are."

We struggled for years to reconcile the popular image of AA and its Twelve Step offspring with the rollicking, irreverent group we attended with our patients. It seemed that for every person we met who talked about having a personal relationship with God, there was another who virtually ignored the issue. We couldn't find much difference in the quality of their respective sobriety. Some of the most mature, good-hearted, altruistic, and principled persons we encountered were atheists and agnostics. And some of the most grasping types. . . . Well, you get the picture.

Later on, we began to encounter splinter groups, where former AA members joined with others to hold Twelve Step–style meetings without the Twelve Steps. The best known of these was a group called Secular Sobriety, founded by James Christopher. Once again, we saw no diminishment of the quality of recovery among members of this group. They helped each other out, offered advice and support, shared their experiences—in short, did everything good AA members do, without mentioning God. They'd left the Twelve Step fold for about the same reasons the colonial settlers had left Europe—freedom to believe what they wanted and to live the way they chose. We certainly couldn't fault them for that.

We began to meet nonbelievers (a generic term for people who don't subscribe to belief in God) among our own patients. One fellow, a physician, made a particular impression on us. Although a practicing atheist, active in the movement against prayer in the schools, he claimed he owed his sobriety to the Twelve Steps of AA. We asked how he reconciled two apparently contradictory beliefs.

"They aren't contradictory at all," he explained. "The Steps aren't commandments, they're *suggestions*. And nobody's saying they were handed down by God; they came from the experience of a bunch of drunks, like me. They're a proven method for staying sober, that's all, and as far as I'm concerned, they work beautifully."

"But what about the references to God in the Steps?" we asked.

"It's always, 'God as we understood Him,' " he replied. "And as far as I understand, God doesn't exist."

"So what do you use for a higher power?"

"The group," he told us. "And my own better nature, as I come into contact with it during the meetings."

After seven productive years in AA, this man began attending Secular Sobriety, and now considers himself a member of both organizations. "Sometimes people from one group or another will pressure me to choose between them," he said. "But I don't see why I should. I get something from both. Besides, I call myself a *free-thinker*, and going to both is what I freely think I should do."

So we decided to write a book for nonbelievers both within and outside of Twelve Step groups, looking at the task of achieving sobriety from the perspective of someone who doesn't accept the notion of God or a higher power. Throughout the book, we will speak from experience. We've been watching nonbelievers recover from addiction for twenty years, and are grateful to have had the opportunity to play some small role in their success. We offer this book as a simple aid to the alcoholic or addict who is trying to recover from addictive disease, yet can't bring himself to accept the spiritual program that has helped so many others. Don't worry about it. It's nothing to regret. There are other options.

One caveat: Experience has taught us that many nonbelievers are, in fact, quite spiritual persons. It's a good illustration of the oft-ignored distinction between spirituality and religion. Specialists in child development tell us that spiritual impulses of one sort or another are found in all human beings, regardless of age, race, culture, education, or personality type. But those leanings are expressed in quite different ways. You don't have to go to church to see the best of humanity in action. When the rescue worker slides hundreds of feet down a crumbling mineshaft to rescue a baby girl—well, he doesn't do that for the salary.

Religion, on the other hand, is simply a *form* spirituality may take. A way of structuring one's spiritual life. Many religions do a great deal of good, but we've all seen how the idea of religion can be perverted to selfish ends—how supposedly altruistic ministries can degenerate into greedy, dangerous cults of personality. It's no accident that the traditions of Alcoholics Anonymous were designed to prevent charismatic individuals from exerting undue influence on its membership.

We did not write this book because we think there's something wrong with people who believe in God. We wrote it because as clinicians, we are sworn to help the addict and alcoholics, believer and nonbeliever alike. Teaching about recovery is our job, and we are simply trying to do it a little better.

In the following pages, we'll discuss the process of addiction, recovery, and the dangers of relapse, from the perspective of the nonbeliever. We've even included a section on how to use a Twelve Step group and the Twelve Steps themselves, without using God as a higher power. There are quite a few such people doing exactly that in America today. And because people who are skeptical about religion are usually skeptical about easy explanations wherever they find them, we've tried to anticipate and answer your questions as fully as we can. Only you can decide whether or not we've succeeded.

Before we begin, let's discuss briefly an issue we'll investigate in more detail in subsequent chapters. That is, the need for a higher power of one sort or another, even for the nonbeliever.

WHY RECOVERY REQUIRES HELP

You may be wondering why we chose the title *Under Your Own Power* when our message is that recovery is difficult or impossible without some kind of assistance. Good question. Here's the answer: We selected that particular title because it emphasizes *your choice*. We're not handing you a "higher power.'" We're saying you should find your own.

Of course, we could have titled the book "Get Sober by Yourself and Tell Everyone Else to Go Jump in the Lake," and probably sold a billion copies to alcoholics who are dying to hear that particular message. But we'd be lying. You can't spend twenty years watching intelligent, strong-willed, and determined individuals utterly ruin their lives by insisting on doing things their own way without reaching that conclusion.

Perhaps this is a good time to explain why people tend to fail when they try to recover by themselves. It helps to think of addiction as a disease of the brain. As dependence develops (see Chapter Six, on the nature of addiction), the nervous system adapts to perceive the drug not as the toxin it is, but rather as a "normalizing agent"—something which actually *improves* brain function by meeting the biochemical needs of the cell. Eventually, the brain reaches a point where it becomes "sick" if the drug is unavailable. The resulting anxiety, nausea, irritability, tremors, insomnia, and craving for the drug compose the *withdrawal syndrome*. In a sense, the nervous system during withdrawal is simply expressing its great displeasure at the sudden absence of the drug to which it has become accustomed.

But it is this same brain, under the influence of addiction, upon which the alcoholic relies to make complex decisions, assess risk and reward, plan the future, guide him through the maze of situations and circumstances which comprise "everyday life." It's not hard to understand how these two agendas become confused. The brain's biochemical need to survive—in other words, to obtain and use the drug it now believes necessary to life itself—undermines or overwhelms other thinking processes. Just as the shark lives to eat, the addicted brain exists to obtain and consume its drug of choice.

Thus the alcoholic, left to his own devices, invariably finds himself back in the firepit of active addiction. Distorted thinking interferes with the ability to monitor and change behavior. Knowingly or unknowingly, the addict follows the biological "instructions" of the addicted brain only to discover (to his amazement) that he is once again in the grip of the disease.

It's a perfect example of the axiom: "We have met the enemy and he is us."

How then can one deal with a will and mind seemingly bent on self-destruction? The answer lies outside oneself. For some, it's found in the Higher Power of AA's Twelve Steps. For others, it's in the group support and cognitive techniques of Rational Recovery. Sometimes the solution is found through the intervention of a trusted counselor or therapist. But the answer is, in one way or another, found somewhere other than in the recesses of your own brain.

But there's a catch: Turning to others, even in time of need, always requires the exercise of faith. When a surgical patient accepts the anesthesia, she shows faith in her doctor. When an astronaut accelerates into space, he exhibits faith in the gigantic machine which bears him toward the moon. Whenever life compels you to trust someone—your accountant, your attorney, your plumber— you exercise faith in something outside yourself.

And you probably hesitate before you do. After all, everyone has personal experience of misplaced faith. Still, as you strive to protect yourself from disappointment, you recognize that sooner or later, you're going to have to trust someone again. There isn't really any alternative.

Especially if you're striving to recover from addiction, and your own feelings undermine you.

We suppose the real issue isn't whether or not you need outside help—you do, if you're going to recover—but who or what that help should be.

In the next chapter, we're going to examine the challenge of finding faith in early recovery. Unlike some authors, we won't try to dictate to you a spiritual program necessary to recovery. Instead, we'll follow the lead of the founders of Alcoholics Anonymous (note we said the *founders*, not all the current members) and give you the freedom to choose your own.

One last comment: we've come to believe that what scares newly sober alcoholics and addicts isn't so much the notion of God or a Higher Power, but the realization that for once in their lives, they can't do it alone. For people who have invested so much in self-control, there are few things more frightening.

But we hope that through the intervention of this book, believers and nonbelievers can stop arguing the existence of a deity long enough to get on with the business of recovery—relying on a power greater than themselves which (wonder of wonders!) might even include one another.

Chapter Two

THE CHALLENGE OF FAITH FOR THE NONBELIEVER

As we were saying: Even if you don't need God to recover, you do need faith.

Nearly everyone concedes the importance of a positive outlook on life, not only in the treatment of addiction but of a variety of serious illnesses. There's nothing abstract about this. During the healing process, there comes a point (or several points) where you as an alcoholic or addict—or victim of cancer, heart, lung, or psychiatric disease—find yourself wanting to chuck treatment and give up. It's natural enough, but it can be quite debilitating. More importantly, this sense of hopelessness doesn't respond to a pat on the back, admonishments to "keep your chin up," or even to antidepressant medicines. To survive, you must find, somewhere in the core of your being, the capacity to *believe* in the future. To assume that somehow, despite your experience up to this point, life is worth going on with. That if you can just hang in there for one more day—even an hour—things will work out.

Logic alone won't carry you to this conclusion. Without a degree of primitive, rudimentary faith, most of us would simply lie down and die. You may have seen some people do just that.

The more desperate your straits, the more you require faith to carry you through. It's no accident that spiritual conversions usually come when life is at ebb tide. These are times when reason clearly isn't enough. To get to the next level, you have to close your eyes and jump—a leap of faith.

Arguments arise, however, over where one's faith should be placed. Should we reach out to God as the evangelists do, praying to be "healed"? Or seek to restore our sanity through the "Power greater than ourselves" described in the Twelve Steps? Perhaps we should reject the notion of a Higher Power altogether, striving instead to assume control of our own destinies through programs such as Rational Recovery or Secular Sobriety. Or enter the labyrinth of psychoanalysis, searching for change in the twists and turns of our own psyches.

No matter which road we choose, the practical application of faith is *always* challenging. In a crisis, it's as difficult for a true believer to place his trust in God as it is for the atheist to exercise his self-discipline. No matter what our beliefs, it is a struggle to adhere to them. At one time or another, faith eludes us all.

A major obstacle to finding faith is the rigid framework within which most of us consider the notion of a higher power. When it comes to spirituality, we must all battle a tendency toward dogmatism. This no doubt stems from the black-or-white, all-or-nothing thinking of childhood, when most of us were introduced to religion. But it's useful to remember that both the atheist and the religious zealot may use a concept of God which is narrow, restricted, and intellectually confining. One simply rejects what the other blindly accepts. Frequently, neither the believer nor the nonbeliever bothers to consider an alternative. It appears as if we would rather be "right" than understand the issues, fight rather than communicate.

One thing is certain: Mankind has always been attracted to the idea of a spiritual power outside himself. Our concept of "God" has altered thousands of times. The spirit world of primitive cultures, with its household idols, was replaced by the sophisticated multideity cosmologies of ancient Egypt, India, China, Greece, and Rome. Ultimately, these beliefs were, in turn, superseded by the "one God" represented in Jewish, Christian, and Islamic theologies.

One reason for the phenomenal growth of Twelve Step fellowships since 1935 was their willingness to abandon a structured model of God in favor of a more flexible, individualized, and inclusive view. This met a need that traditional religions did not. Groups such as Secular Sobriety came into existence because some recovering persons found even AA's loose spirituality too confining. Yet adherents of all approaches recognize the human need for faith.

Perhaps it would help to compare and contrast these different approaches in terms of their impact on recovery from alcoholism or drug dependence. To make this easier, we've grouped them into three larger schools of thought, or "models." Each offers its own explanation of the nature and origins of God, and of the relationship between God and the recovering alcoholic. As we discuss them in turn, note their differences and similarities.

THE TRADITIONAL DEITY MODEL: GOD IS EVERYTHING

Most of the world's organized religions personify God as a deity with a specific agenda for humankind and for the universe as a whole. Only part of this agenda may have been revealed to Man; as to the rest, we are largely in the dark. God is therefore portrayed as omniscient, omnipotent, omnipresent—in other words, everything human beings are not.

Ironically, this all-powerful deity may also be invested by the faithful with decidedly human traits: the jealous nature of God in the Old Testament, for example, versus the merciful deity of the Gospels. Likewise, most of us who were raised in conventional churches learned to emphasize one aspect or another of God's imaginary "personality." Perhaps we saw God as angry, punitive, unforgiving; maybe God seemed gentle and tolerant of our failures. In either case, we visualize God in human form—majestic, perhaps, but still one of us.

In one sense, the popularity of the deity model actually accounts for the rise of atheism. That's because in strictly human terms, God's greatest creation, the world, is a disaster. Think about it: Can you accept the notion of an all-seeing, all-knowing, all-powerful God who would nevertheless create a universe full of starvation, natural catastrophe, injustice, cruelty, and wanton destruction? Where the only reward came after death?

What's the point? As one fellow put it: "If there is a God, He ought to be shot."

As we grow up, many of us come to reject the picture of God that has been in our heads since childhood. We're no longer satisfied to think of God as a super- Dad or Mom figure, whose essentially erratic and unpredictable behavior requires constant rationalization. Of course, some of us reject the notion of God outright, earning the label "atheist." But even atheists often believe in a power greater than themselves—it just isn't the God they knew as children, see portrayed in church, or read about in the Bible.

THE DEITY MODEL AND THE RECOVERING PERSON

For those alcoholics and addicts who continue to think of God as the deity portrayed by their religion, the path to salvation is simple. They must find their way back to God. He, being omnipotent, can restore the addict to sanity. But His methods may be inscrutable: God, after all, is beyond the understanding of Man. Thus recovery usually comes through the *conversion experience:* God reaches out to touch the alcoholic, removing forever the compulsion to drink. It's magical, sudden, and for the faithful, it often works.

Sobriety, then, is something God does to the alcoholic or addict as part and parcel of a general transformation of character. All credit naturally belongs to God. As is so often the case in deity-based theology, the individual's role is receptive, even passive.

Which brings us to the other side of the equation: Does God expect anything in return? It's a difficult question. Since God *is* everything, He obviously needs nothing from humankind, except perhaps worship, and obedience to His commandments. Straying from the path of God presumably leads to tragedy. It's no surprise that many Western religions advise the faithful that alcoholism itself is a form of spiritual punishment for abandoning the church.

The deity model works very well as a basis for religion, but from the standpoint of recovery, it has an important flaw. The true conversion experience doesn't occur often enough to make a dent in the larger population of alcoholics. For every addict who sees the light and devotes his life to God, there are dozens more who would rather die than submit to the paternalistic deity of their childhood.

Worse yet, even those whose faith seems absolute may never feel the hand of God releasing them from addiction.

Clearly, those afflicted with the disease of alcoholism needed something to replace the conventional deity model as a linchpin for faith. The Twelve Steps helped to meet this need by redefining the notion of God.

THE TWELVE STEP MODEL: GOD OF OUR UNDERSTANDING

The nature of the Higher Power in the Twelve Steps is substantially different from that described in traditional religions. In many ways, the Twelve Step concept of a spiritual power reflects the diverse attitudes of the original membership of Alcoholics Anonymous. Recall that many early members of AA were "dropouts" from a variety of faiths, particularly the Roman Catholic Church. Some (including Bill Wilson, one of AA's two founders) had themselves undergone the classic conversion experience. Others were agnostics; a vocal minority were determined atheists. Remember, too, that early AA relied on consensus of opinion (the most inefficient form of governance) to make important decisions. It was inevitable that the role of God became the subject of heated debate within the fledgling fellowship.

The language of the Steps themselves (especially use of the terms "Power greater than ourselves" and "God as we understood Him") reflects the intensity of this controversy and the need to reach a compromise that members could accept. Unlike conventional religion, the Twelve Steps allow one to pray either to God or to another, alternative Higher Power that mirrors your own beliefs. It seems confusing until you realize that the second and third Steps are designed not to direct you one way or another but to give you a *choice* between a higher power of your preference and the traditional "high*est* power" (God).

STEP TWO: Came to believe that a Power greater than ourselves could restore us to sanity.

STEP THREE: Made a decision to turn our will and our lives over to the care of God *as we understood Him*.

In turn, the Higher Power of the Steps is often depicted as all-*encompassing* rather than omnipotent. Anything which seeks to meet the needs of the highly diverse membership of Twelve Step groups must be very flexible, unencumbered with dogma. In AA, all concepts of the Higher Power are valid as long as they reflect the sincere belief of the individual.

Thus, the Higher Power originates not in church dogma but in the understanding and experience of the alcoholic. Accordingly, it may or may not conform to the Judeo-Christian or Muslim model of the one God. From the nonbeliever's standpoint, the principle advantage of the Step approach is its inclusiveness, which leaves room even for the atheist and agnostic.

As Twelve Steppers sometimes put it: "We don't ask you to believe in God. We just ask you to admit that *you're not* God."

THE TWELVE STEP MODEL AND THE RECOVERING PERSON

The Higher Power's role is to assist you in adopting the principles outlined in the Twelve Steps ("to practice these principles in all our affairs.") There's an important distinction to make here. Though alcoholics enter AA to stop drinking, they quickly learn that recovery involves more than just giving up alcohol and drugs. The secret is to learn to live differently: by principles rather than personality, self-knowledge instead of denial, faith rather than ambition. Success comes from sticking with the program ("Rarely have we seen someone fail who has thoroughly followed our path."), and the change which occurs, though less spectacular than the conversion experience, is every bit as far-reaching.

Broadly stated, the Steps suggest you:

Admit powerlessness over addiction: Acknowledging that you have lost control over chemicals and that your life has become unmanageable sets the stage for the entrance of the Higher Power, who can help you do what you haven't been able to accomplish on your own.

Assume faith in a Higher Power: You accept the need for outside assistance in recovery, forsaking further attempts to beat your addiction through willpower.

Abandon insistence on personal control: You turn your will and life over to whatever outside power you believe in.

Examine yourself: You study your own behavior (often quite a change from an earlier preoccupation with criticizing others) in terms of right and wrong.

Make personal changes: You become willing to have your Higher Power remedy these character defects.

Make amends to those you harmed: You seek to atone for the wrongs of the past where possible.

Pray and Meditate: You ask your Higher Power for guidance (prayer) and promise to listen to and reflect on the answers (meditation).

Carry the message: You share your experience with those who still suffer, as a way of reinforcing the message in your own thinking.

Obviously, this is quite different from traditional religious dogma. It's a way of thinking and acting designed to lead to a degree of personal serenity. Though some Twelve Step meetings seem dogmatic to newcomers—especially nonbelievers, and justifiably so—that's usually the result of dogmatic individuals within the fellowship itself rather than any innate rigidity in the Steps. After all, it's human nature (however unfortunate) to foist one's beliefs upon others. Twelve Steppers strive to acknowledge their imperfections, promising only to make progress in the search for self-knowledge and a moral life.

FAITH IN THE CHRONIC DISEASE MODEL:
WHATEVER WORKS

As flexible as the Twelve Step model may be, there are still plenty of alcoholics and addicts who find it too confining. Thus, we in the treatment field have made further changes in our thinking.

Those who believe, as we do, that addiction represents a chronic disease, recognize the value, even the necessity, of faith in the recovery process. Yet we don't feel compelled to restrict our patients to any one spiritual program. Instead, we hold that the best criteria for judging the quality of a spiritual approach is simply that it *works*. Any method that leads to sobriety and peace of mind is, in our book, perfectly legitimate.

After all, something that helps you do what you've previously failed to do (recover from addiction) is obviously worth attention. We place only one condition on your Higher Power: It must always be something other than yourself.

We explained the reasoning behind this in the opening chapter. As an addict, your thinking has been influenced to the point where you have become your own worst enemy—your desires and decisions usually undermine recovery rather than facilitate it. You must look elsewhere for the answers you need.

From our perspective, a *Higher Power* is anything outside yourself which helps you learn to live with the disease. Your role is to seek out guidance, and then pay attention to the advice you're given.

In fact, your Higher Power may change substantially as you move through the various stages of treatment. Here's an example: Bill, a chronic alcoholic and addict with many objections to organized religion, nonetheless uses one "higher power" after another to get him from one phase of recovery to the next. Without acknowledging a concept of God, Bill is still able to place his faith where it will help him the most.

Initial Stage: Bill came to the hospital through an intervention involving his family and employer. Although aware of his problem with alcohol, he admitted he would never have sought treatment on his own because of fear he would lose his job as a police officer. His first few days in detox were painful, and he required extra doses of medication to suppress his tremors. He wanted to leave the hospital several times during the first two days, but was held back by the prospect of losing his job.

Higher Power in the Initial Stage: Bill's first "HP" was his family. Their concern and confrontation overcame his fear of asking for help. His second "HP" was the knowledge that if he left treatment, he would find himself unemployed and unable to finance his drinking. Even the tranquilizers given by his doctor qualified as a Higher Power of sorts; without them, he might have bolted the hospital despite the consequences.

Rehabilitation Stage: Bill went on to complete an inpatient program of approximately three weeks duration. During the period Bill bonded strongly with the other patients; they convinced him to stay for the entire program, and he even found himself convincing newer patients not to give up hope. Though Bill objected to reliance on God, he could see the importance of involvement in AA as a way of getting support for sobriety after he left the hospital. As a nonbeliever, Bill also attended meetings of Secular Sobriety, and found them helpful.

Higher Power in the Rehab Stage: Without the assistance of the patient group itself, and the encouragement of recovering alcoholics he meets at Alcoholics Anonymous and Secular Sobriety meetings, Bill would probably have returned to drinking. Again, though Bill struggles with the language of AA, he is able to *set aside* his objections long enough to benefit from other aspects of the fellowship. That's characteristic of reliance on a Higher Power: You go past obstacles rather than becoming "stuck" trying to solve one problem or another. Ironically, many of the problems that worry Bill most at this point in his recovery—unpaid bills, a lawsuit that won't end, arguments with his wife, fear of losing his job—will simply clear up by themselves, given time and sobriety. Had Bill insisted on "resolving" each issue, he might well have failed, and given himself an excuse to return to drinking.

Aftercare stage: After discharge, Bill involves himself in meetings and participates in a structured aftercare program that meets twice weekly at the hospital where he underwent treatment.

Higher Power in Aftercare: Bill maintains his contacts with the treatment program but begins to transfer his reliance to the Secular Sobriety and Twelve Step meetings where he feels comfortable. His objections to the religious content of AA are largely a thing of the past, because he's found a workable alternative. He didn't resolve these issues; he moved beyond them.

Maintenance Stage: Bill completes aftercare and continues his involvement in both AA and Secular Sobriety.

Higher Power in the Maintenance Stage: Bill still doesn't believe in any concept of God, but feels the "wisdom of the group" of recovering alcoholics keeps him sober. That's a higher power by our definition.

ARE YOU A "REASONER" OR A "REACTOR"?

There are two broad categories of nonbelievers. One type arrives at a position of philosophical skepticism following a period of reflection, study, and analysis. As a result, he usually seems quite comfortable with himself, and tolerant towards the differing views of others.

The second sort derives his skepticism not from logic but from negative feelings about God, organized religion, and the people who (in his mind, at least) represent it. It's not hard to spot this type. They are, in the words of one observer, "pissed off at the world, and at God for making it."

The first nonbeliever (whom we'll dub the "Reasoner") distrusts his own strong emotions, seeking always a rational basis for action.

The second type (we'll call him the "Emotional Reactor") uses his intellect to defend his angry feelings. Underneath, he's a volcano.

There's an interesting twist. While the Reasoner may view himself as overemotional (and isn't), the Emotional Reactor often sees himself as cool and intellectual. In reality, he's quite the opposite.

Here's a nonbeliever (named Fred) being interviewed by his counselor. See if you can figure out which type he is.

FRED: I just want you to know right off the bat, I'm not going to AA, because I'm not interested in that God stuff.

COUNSELOR: Okay.

FRED: I mean, I've heard you people insist on AA, and if that's true, I'm leaving.

COUNSELOR: We have another group here called S.O.S. which doesn't mention a Higher Power.

FRED: Good. Because I've had enough nagging from my wife about God. She's a religious fanatic.

COUNSELOR: Really? You mean born again?

FRED: No, of course not, but she goes to church, and she only drinks once a week, if that often.

COUNSELOR: Doesn't sound like a fanatic to me.

FRED: Well, you know what I mean. So don't ask me to read any of that AA literature or anything. Understand?

COUNSELOR: Perfectly. Okay, now about your recent sleep patterns . . .

FRED: Because if you do, I'm leaving.

COUNSELOR: Fred, would you like to discuss your feelings about God, or about AA?

FRED: No! That's precisely what I don't want to discuss!

COUNSELOR: You keep bringing it up.

FRED: No I don't. You do.

COUNSELOR: All right. Why exactly do you dislike AA so much? Have you ever been?

FRED: No, but I know all about it. Don't get me wrong, I don't have anything against those people, but they're just too emotional for me. I'm the intellectual type. If you want me to do

something, give me a reason. But don't talk to me about God. I
don't wanna hear it.
COUNSELOR: No problem.
FRED: Because if you do . . .

Fred's aggressive rejection of AA springs not from a philosophical
stance of religious nonbelief, but more likely from his anger at being
in treatment for alcoholism. And his approach is based on pure
emotion, rather than the intellect he trumpets. It's a "hook" on
which he can hang his resistance to the treatment process. If another patient mentions God in a group, Fred may even use that as an
excuse to leave the program against the advice of his doctor.

Notice how different that is from the position taken by Boris,
another patient in the same treatment center.

COUNSELOR: I notice you describe yourself as an atheist. Any
problems with AA?
BORIS: I don't really know. I've never been. I've heard there's a lot
of religion involved.
COUNSELOR: They talk about a Higher Power, and a God of your
understanding. But it's pretty loose, and I know a lot of atheists
and agnostics who go to meetings.
BORIS: If I'm not comfortable with it after a few meetings, is
there any other group I could attend?
COUNSELOR: Sure, we have an S.O.S. group here. Similar, but no
spiritual stuff.
BORIS: Let me give it a try.

It's apparent that Boris is striving to recover without religion,
while Fred is using his religious objections to excuse his resistance to
treatment. Thus, Fred's "nonbelief" is really symptomatic of denial,
and thus part of this disease, while Boris's attitude is philosophically
sound and merits respect.

Which are you? If you'd like some honest feedback, present your
views to other recovering people, and ask them: do I seem to have
reasoned this out, or do I seem angry and basing my responses on
my anger?

WATCH OUT FOR FALSE GODS

A word of warning: Even the most dedicated atheist is still vulnerable to the lure of "false gods" or gurus, who lead you in the wrong direction entirely. Here's an example.

"LOWER POWER"

Addicts, like most people in trouble, are attracted to anything that promises a quick, easy solution to their problems. Unfortunately, experience tells us no such solution exists. But there's no shortage of counselors, therapists, and advisors who will tell you it *does*, usually in return for large sums of cash. We couldn't begin to count the number of alcoholics who have wasted years struggling to maintain sobriety using methods that simply do not work. We call such false hope the work of a Lower Power: an outside influence whose guidance helps you spin your wheels, or actually drags you down.

A Lower Power usually takes the form of an individual or group which promises help or even a cure for your addiction. Especially noteworthy are those which do not require abstinence, instead permitting the alcoholic or addict to remain in "treatment" despite multiple relapses. Often this complicity with failure is justified by the claim that the relapser is "working" on some underlying psychological issue. Here's a news flash: if you're an alcoholic, the only issue of importance in early recovery is whether or not you had a drink today.

Lower Powers spring from the desire of sick alcoholics and addicts for magical answers to long-standing problems—especially any solution that doesn't involve giving up alcohol. Even well-intentioned therapists can be lured into the role of secular *guru* by their own secret desire to "rescue" or cure their patients.

You can tell you're involved with a Lower Power because you won't get better. Oh, you may improve in some areas—perhaps you'll understand some aspect of your childhood, or improve communication skills—but overall, your life will continue to deteriorate. You'll have to convince yourself that therapy is helping in the face of mounting evidence that it isn't. This sort of self-delusion is easier if your guru has a powerful, attractive personality; that's why some of the most charismatic figures in psychology have fallen into the role of Lower Power for their alcoholic or addicted patients.

You'll keep trying, you'll keep failing, you'll keep paying. In fact, you won't really make any progress until you *drop out* of therapy and begin to tackle the real task of sobriety.

Ben's Story

Watch as Ben misplaces his faith in a "lower power."

Ben realized he had a problem with cocaine shortly before he filed his first Chapter 11 bankruptcy petition. Frightened by his recent losses, he asked his best friend, who was also his attorney, for advice.

"Call this doctor," his friend advised, writing a phone number on a piece of paper. "He was the guy Bill Smith went to."

"Smith? Wasn't he that dude that got arrested for insider trading?"

His friend nodded. "A stone cokehead. And he says this guy put him in a program, turned his life around."

Ben took the number, but secretly rebelled against the idea of seeing a doctor. *I'm not that bad, for Christ's sake. I haven't been arrested or anything.* And they'd probably make him attend some meetings of religious fanatics. *There's got to be an alternative. Something* reasonable, *for Pete's sake. That's all I ask.*

A few days later he saw an advertisement for a weekend seminar, entitled "Becoming Your Own Master: An Experience in Self-Esteem." *That's what I really need,* he told himself. *Better self-esteem.*

The seminar was, in Ben's eyes, a life-changing experience. He was entranced by the leader's presentation, overcome by the feelings he experienced in the exercises. He left with a renewed sense of self-worth and the conviction that he could handle whatever problems arose.

A week later, he received notification of his bankruptcy hearing. He set the notice down on his desk, left the office, purchased three grams of cocaine, bought a bottle of 151 proof rum, and went on a twenty-four-hour binge.

After he recovered from his hangover, Ben called the center that sponsored the seminar he'd attended and asked for a private consultation with the seminar leader.

"My friend," the leader said after Ben told his story, "you don't have a drug problem. You have a living problem."

"Really?"

"Absolutely. I'm going to sign you up in our special seminar, "Becoming Your Own Behavior Therapist," which meets next month. That should do the trick."

"How long does it last?"

"One week, residential, at our Life Change Center in New Brunford."

"A week?" Ben gulped. "I'll have to cancel my appointments."

"Do it. If you're not worth it, what is?"

The seminar was indeed terrific. Ben loved the feeling of being nurtured by the group, of belonging, of being bombarded with new insights. Yet he was bothered by persistent cocaine dreams all through the week. Shortly after his return, he went on yet another bender, this one lasting nearly three days and causing him to miss an important meeting with his creditors.

Remorseful and depressed, Ben scheduled another session with the seminar leader. "Ben, Ben," the leader said, shaking his head sadly. "You're resisting the program. You're not applying the principles. I'm beginning to question your motivation."

"I really want to succeed. I really do."

"I believe you, Ben. I think what you need is our intensive seminar, "Becoming Your Own Incentive Plan," which meets in California in February. That's only two weeks away. I'll register you."

"California?" Ben said weakly. "Plane fare extra?"

"Ben," the leader said. "If you're not worth it . . ."

"I know, I know. What is."

Ben once again enjoyed the seminar, although his pleasure was tainted by his earlier experiences with relapse. He lasted nearly a month following his return. The subsequent binges—three within a six-week period, each more devastating than the last—resulted in his arrest for drunk driving and leaving the scene of an accident. He met with his attorney after his release.

"I don't understand why you didn't call the doctor whose name I gave you," the lawyer said irritably.

"Oh, what was he gonna do?" Ben whined. "Tell me not to do coke and go to meetings?"

"Which is exactly what you *should* do, Benjamin."

"But what good does quitting coke do if I'm still not happy?"

"It would keep you out of debt, out of court, and out of jail," the attorney said. "I don't know why that's not enough. And you don't even need plane fare to do it."

ADDICTION'S TEN COMMANDMENTS

There's a paradox involved in being an alcoholic or addict who is also a nonbeliever. Addiction itself bears many of the trappings of religious sects: ritualistic behavior, ecstatic experiences, strict codes of conduct, even martyrdom. In that sense, all addicts belong to a "religion" of sorts, even if they don't realize it. To carry our metaphor to its logical endpoint, we offer you our impression of "Ten Commandments" for the faithful followers of an imaginary Church of the Exalted Chemical. See if they don't reflect the reality of the addictive lifestyle.

THE FIRST COMMANDMENT:

THOU SHALT HAVE NO OTHER GODS BEFORE THE DRUG

Think of all the alcoholics who have sacrificed career, family, fortune, and even life itself in the service of the Great God Alcohol. And what did they receive in return? A few moments of relief from psychic and physical pain, which was probably brought on by the drug in the first place.

Has a more "jealous" god ever existed? Not content with the devotion of evenings and weekends, alcohol and drugs eventually demand morning prayers, as well (often conducted while kneeling over the toilet bowl). No corrupt television evangelist ever bilked his followers for a greater share of their earnings than cocaine. No holy war ever took a greater toll on human life than alcohol and drugs.

THE SECOND COMMANDMENT:

THOU SHALT HONOR THE DRUG BEFORE THY FATHER AND MOTHER

Doesn't devotion to the drug supersede family loyalties? Children steal from their parents to get drugs, then weep with shame in treatment programs. Husbands leave their wives, wives forsake their husbands, parents abandon their kids to strangers, children run away to live on the streets—all in the name of the "right" to consume alcohol or drugs.

THE THIRD COMMANDMENT:

THOU SHALT KILL ANY WHO THREATEN THE DRUG

Five years ago, this would have been an exaggeration. But that was before armed kids roamed poor neighborhoods, and dealers carried Uzis, and random violence claimed as many victims as intentional homicide. Maybe people don't kill for alcohol, but that's probably because they don't have to. It's everywhere. Recall, however, the days of Prohibition . . .

THE FOURTH COMMANDMENT:

THOU SHALT SACRIFICE THY CHILDREN TO ME

Have any idea how many children are born with Fetal Alcohol Syndrome because their mothers drank during pregnancy? Or how many infants must be detoxified from heroin or cocaine in the nursery?

THE FIFTH COMMANDMENT:

THOU SHALT SET ASIDE TIME TO WORSHIP ME

How many alcoholics limit themselves during the week, only to binge on the weekends? Or swear off alcohol for Lent (usually to prove that he/she "can't" be an alcoholic), only to return to drinking as soon as the holiday ends?

THE SIXTH COMMANDMENT:

THOU SHALT NOT QUESTION ME

Isn't it amazing how normally intelligent men and women become blind to the obvious effects of alcohol and drugs? A man called us recently with this request: "I demand a thorough, objective, and unbiased evaluation by an expert to prove once and for all that I am *not* an alcoholic." Now there's an open mind for you.

THE SEVENTH COMMANDMENT:

THOU SHALT SUSPECT EVERYONE BUT ME

What about the cocaine addict who questioned health advice of his physician but not his dealer. "The doctors try to tell you coke is bad for your heart, but Eduardo swears it lowers your blood pressure." Or the near-terminal alcoholic who insists her family's only motive for trying to get her into detox is "just to kill me off so they can get their grubby hands on my money." If they'd wanted her to die, they need only leave her to her own devices. Few people commit suicide more effectively than a drinking alcoholic.

THE EIGHTH COMMANDMENT:

THOU SHALT SEEK FORGIVENESS ONLY THROUGH ME

At last aware of all he's lost through drinking, gripped by shame and remorse, does the alcoholic turn to friends, confidants, God? No—most seek relief from still more alcohol, as though after all these years, that path finally led to something besides still more pain.

THE NINTH COMMANDMENT:

THOU SHALT NOT FORGET ME

Even years after the last drink, the last hit, the last dose, the drug seeks to call the faithful to worship. Cravings and vivid dreams of drinking and using live forever in the recesses of the brain, like the

Sirens' song. "You can't live without me," the drug calls, even as it kills you.

THE TENTH COMMANDMENT:

THOU SHALT MAKE OFFERINGS TO ME

A minority of the congregation contributes the bulk of donations to most churches. But then, about 10 percent of drinkers consume more than 50 percent of alcoholic beverages. So who's more devoted?

Want to compare houses of worship? Open the Yellow Pages and count the number of churches. Now count the number of bars, grills, package stores, and restaurants that serve alcohol.

How about tithing? Call your local church and ask how much was contributed through the collection plate in the past year. Now call a successful drinking establishment and ask how much they earned from selling liquor.

You tell us: Which god is most honored in our culture?

Chapter Three

TEN MILESTONES ON THE ROAD TO RECOVERY

AS A NONBELIEVER, chances are you have made a conscious choice at some point in your life to reject popular notions of God and religion. Many nonbelievers are put on the defensive early by our society—there's no getting around the fact that Judeo-Christian ideology is engrained in Western culture. A lifetime of maintaining and perhaps professing beliefs that differ from the norm lead nonbelievers to develop a nature that is tenacious to some, stubborn to others. The skepticism applied to spiritual questions often colors the way a nonbeliever approaches every issue. While this hard-fought skepticism may be healthy in certain arenas, it can easily become a dangerous obstacle when dealing with the disease of addiction.

Despite remarkable differences in background and personality, addicts and alcoholics follow a fairly predictable path from drinking and drug use to stable abstinence, regardless of whether or not they believe in God. We've marked this path with ten "milestones" you may use as guideposts on your own road to recovery. The order may vary, but not by much. Which milestone marks your progress to this point?

37

FIGURE 3-1

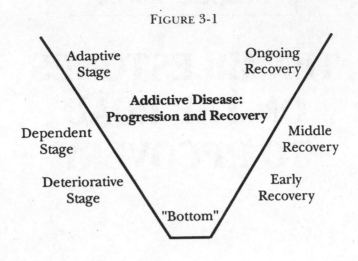

Adaptive Stage
Experimentation reinforced by feeling of euphoria
Recreational use without apparent problems
Signs of elevated tolerance
Learns to use substance to enhance performance
Loss of control absent or rare
Preoccupation with using and obtaining substance
Difficulty enjoying self without aid of substance
Anxiety, irritability, or insomnia when substance unavailable
Integrates substance use into daily or weekly routine
Associates primarily with other substance users
Becomes defensive about substance use
Establishes codependent relationships with others
Cognitive and intellectual deficits from substance use begin

Dependent Stage
Onset of obvious withdrawal: tremor, nausea, sleeplessness
Drug or alcohol use primarily *medicinal*, not recreational
Increase in amount or frequency of consumption
Signs of loss of control over amount, time and place, duration of
    episode
Increasing reliance on defense mechanisms to explain away
    problems

Further restricts self to associations with heavy drinkers, users, or codependents
May seek psychological or medical help for "phantom disorders"
Deliberately misleads others about use
Rationalizes behavior as "normal" and dismisses complaints as "overreaction"
Increasingly preoccupied with own discomfort and neglectful of others
Greater distortion of thinking, loses touch with reality
Cognitive and intellectual deficits worsen; memory deteriorates
Enters "toxic" state: personality distorted by brain dysfunction

Deteriorative Stage
Overt conflicts with others about substance-related problems
Obvious legal, social, marital, medical, occupational, financial problems
"Binge" consumption
Unpredictable behavior
Extreme personality disfigurement; "Jekyll and Hyde"
Physician interventions and hospital visits
Acute medical emergencies
Accidents or other driving related difficulties
Threat of job loss
Threat of marital separation or loss of family
Increasing isolation; drug becomes "only friend" remaining

Early Recovery
Seeks help for alcohol/drug problems
Enters to alleviate outside pressure or crisis
Medically detoxified
Brain begins to clear
Distorted thinking begins to abate
Feels angry or resistant towards treatment
Worries about stigma of addiction
Emotionally labile, easily upset
Minimizes extent and severity of history of drug and alcohol use

Middle Recovery

Learns addiction is a disease
Begins to assume responsibility for participation in treatment
Lets go of misplaced shame for being addicted
Feels less isolated; begins to communicate with peers
Relief at having opportunity to recover
Anxiety over possibility of relapse
Anger subsides; stops blaming others for problems

Ongoing Recovery

Active participation in self-help group
Takes personal responsibility for sobriety
Helps others in order to help self
Adopts "unconditional abstinence" as motto
Becomes willing to go to any lengths to remain sober
Beginning feelings of gratitude for help received
Makes sobriety number one priority
Maintains program of ongoing recovery

THE FIRST MILESTONE: SEEKING OUTSIDE HELP

Look at the illustration of the course of addiction and recovery on the opposite page. Note that the first step on the upward curve involves seeking outside assistance. There's a reason for that. In nearly every instance, the sick alcoholic has resisted, avoided, or postponed seeking help from others. Why? For three simple reasons:

1) **Addicts are mistrustful.** A nonbeliever's skepticism isn't only pointed at religion—a strong questioning nature leads nonbelievers to accept little at face value. Imagine what happens when a non-believer joins the ranks of the addict—there's probably no less trusting group on the face of the earth. In fact, many addicts, believers and nonbelievers alike, are clinically paranoid, the result not only of long-term assault on key areas of the brain but also of a lifestyle devoted to concealment, deceit, and even outright lying.

After months or years of manipulating others in order to gain access to drugs or protect himself from the consequences of drug use, the addict may assume that everyone else's motives are as self-serving as his own.

When confronted by his boss, employee assistance counselor, or spouse, he thinks: "They're just trying to get rid of me. Once they get me locked up in one of those places, they'll (*choose one*: fire me, demote me, tell everyone at work where I am, file for divorce, force me to go to AA meetings and pray)."

2) **Addicts have a misplaced belief in willpower.** To an outsider, the addict may appear weak-willed. In reality, he or she is a perfect example of willpower misdirected. Addiction perverts otherwise admirable traits such as ingenuity, salesmanship, and strength of conviction into the obstinance, defensiveness, and manipulation which characterize alcoholic behavior. Willpower, normally a sign of inner strength, gets channeled into endless attempts at hiding the disease of addiction from others, and from oneself. Addiction transforms willpower into arrogance, leading the addict to shun the possibility of looking to others for help. This arrogance is especially prevalent in nonbelievers, who, when told to seek a "higher power" for solace or direction, at first refuse to look anywhere but within themselves, thinking, "If I've got problems, I'm the only one smart enough to fix them." The nonbeliever is "ideologically opposed" to any program that would have him reveal himself to a group of recovering addicts. Such a scenario would force him to humbly place his faith in a collaborative effort to fight his disease, to have faith in something outside of himself. By appealing to his skepticism, he comes up with the perfect excuse to keep drinking or using.

But what the addict ignores is the physiological fact that the disease of addiction takes the mind once strong enough to wield an honorable measure of skepticism and turns it against itself. The brain which the alcoholic insists can handle his problems long ago became the first and most important casualty of the disease. Thus, most addicts engage in a "war" with their own bodies, trying to overcome compulsion through renewed determination and a proliferation of strategies to avoid further problems. One former patient (a psychologist) convinced himself that he drank a case of beer a day simply because it was in the house. "If I purchase no more than two cans at a time," he reasoned, "and force myself to walk three blocks to the store in order to buy them, that will limit my consumption." Of course, by the end of the month, he was making fifteen trips to the store every day. This is not unlike the smoker who switches to a low-tar, low-nicotine brand but doubles his consumption of cigarettes.

Remember the axiom: "We have met the enemy, and he is us."

3) **Even when they know help is needed, addicts put it off.** When it comes to quitting drinking, every alcoholic is a procrastinator. In fact, one of the best known books on alcoholism is entitled *I'll Quit Tomorrow.* Of course, tomorrow never comes. The nonbeliever, sure that stubbornness is a virtue, makes herself believe that she is courageously warding off that abstinent tomorrow, that her natural tenacity will eventually enable her to take control over her drinking or using all by herself. But stubbornness in the face of a debilitating disease is precisely what keeps you from seeking the help you desperately need.

We must recall that to someone who is addicted to a drug, abstinence is, at least initially, a painful process. There's the discomfort of withdrawal. The anxiety of trying to live without alcohol after years of dependence. The fear that people will look down on you because of your past problems. The need to find new friends, new interests, perhaps a new career. The prospect of filling the yawning hole in your daily schedule, once devoted to finding, using, and recovering from drugs. Your doubts about your ability to sleep or relax or perform sexually without chemicals. Will people ever forgive you for the transgressions of the past? And what if you relapse? Does that mean you're a failure?

It's no wonder people put this off. *Maybe I better give this some more thought,* you tell yourself. *Don't want to do something rash.*

In fact, most alcoholics and addicts seek help only under duress: a crisis at work, at home, in health, with the law. The motivation may be no more complicated than the desire to avoid suffering. In some cases, the alcoholic's resistance to help is so great that concerned family members must stage an *intervention*—an organized effort to convince someone to enter treatment, under the direction of a professional—simply to get the alcoholic to see the obvious. We'll never forget watching an innocent nine-year-old patiently explain the symptoms of alcoholism to her father, a surgeon who couldn't understand why everybody was so upset about his occasional three or four day disappearances, fueled by half-gallons of cheap vodka. "But honey, you don't understand," he told her seriously. "Daddy isn't an alcoholic. He's just under a lot of stress."

Once in treatment, however, the process of change develops a momentum of its own. Denial diminishes, is replaced by new knowledge; the illusion of control has been removed. Even if he relapses for brief periods, the addict will never again be entirely comfortable with drinking or drug use. Thus, the saying sometimes heard at meetings of Alcoholics Anonymous: "If nothing else, this will ruin your drinking."

But Where Do I Find Help?

A good question. Many alcoholics and addicts do very well simply by involving themselves in Twelve Step groups or other self-help fellowships. But that's doing it the hard way. Twelve Step organizations work on a principle of "attraction rather than promotion," and it's easy for a newcomer to attend meetings without making any meaningful contact. Groups like Rational Recovery are usually smaller, but most people attend only once weekly, which for many of us simply isn't enough to remain sober. And if you can't establish sobriety fairly quickly, you'll drop out altogether. You may not want to, but you will. It's that simple.

Bill W., one of AA's founders, is reported to have said that although AA was the best way to stay sober, it wasn't necessarily the best way to *get* sober. He was referring to the difficulty of going through withdrawal while keeping up your daily responsibilities and, at the same time, beginning the process of restructuring your life from one built around drinking or drug use to one conducive to sobriety—all with no more support than you can obtain from attending meetings. For every AA member who succeeded, there was another who failed, at least temporarily. This led to a renewed role for professional treatment, including the inpatient and outpatient programs in your community. Most recovering persons eventually become members of a self-help group. Before anything else, regardless of the behavioral strategies used to get you to stop drinking or using, a treatment program must view addiction as a disease. The purpose of treatment is primarily to initiate the recovery process: to detoxify you, teach you about the disease, get you started on the right path, help you over the bumps.

But how do you identify a good treatment program? Shop for it as if you were purchasing a used car instead of a new one. When you search for a used (excuse us, "previously owned") auto, you never take anything at face value, because everyone knows they often have hidden defects. You may like the way a car looks or handles, but if you're wise, you'll still bring it to a mechanic for testing before you buy it. When you purchase a new model, on the other hand, you assume that the car is in good shape and that any undiscovered problems will be covered under the warranty. You, therefore, shop principally for style, color, and price.

With addictions treatment, style and looks are a poor indicator of quality, and no warranties are available.

The same holds true for price. When you purchase an expensive suit, you assume its expense is justified by superior workmanship or design. You might also assume that the most expensive hospitals or treatment programs provide the best, most comprehensive services. Not so. Expense often has little or nothing to do with quality. We're familiar with a treatment program which charges its victims (excuse us, patients) one thousand dollars a day. Yet the counselors and nurses who provide the bulk of the treatment are paid average wages. Why is the program so expensive? Because someone (not the staff) is making a heck of a profit.

Here are eight simple things to look for when shopping for quality treatment.

1. **The program treats addiction as a biogenic disease.** Biogenic means caused by physiological adaptations, as opposed to psychological problems (psychogenic). A program or therapist oriented to a psychogenic approach will probably attribute alcoholic drinking to a need to "self-medicate" underlying emotional problems or to "mask"

or "cope" with unresolved issues from childhood. It's just our opinion—you're free to do whatever you think best—but when we hear terms like these, we run in the opposite direction.

2. **The treatment is aimed at achieving specific goals.** Bad therapists or treatment programs are notoriously vague about the goals of therapy, which leaves them free to interpret failure as success. As one starry-eyed psychiatrist put it, "The great thing about analysis is that you know you're doing the right thing, even if the patient isn't getting better."

What are the appropriate goals? Try these four:

1. The addict should receive education about the disease, so that he or she can understand the directions for treatment.
2. He or she should self-diagnose—that is, recognize the symptoms of disease in past experience.
3. He or she should be introduced to effective methods for maintaining long-term sobriety.
4. He or she should be taught the importance of taking personal responsibility for recovery.

Sound simple? Take our word for it, a treatment program which helps you accomplish those four goals is worth its weight in gold. And one which doesn't is worthless, no matter how beautiful the grounds or prestigious the reputation.

3. **The program emphasizes education.** There's a lot to learn about alcoholism and drug dependence, and nobody needs the information like an alcoholic or drug addict. Nonetheless, many counselors take a deliberately anti-intellectual stance, insisting that participants operate totally on a "gut" level. Believe us, your gut has no special ability to help you stop drinking. Learn all you can about your illness, and ignore anyone who tells you it isn't important.

4. **The program makes use of group therapy.** Groups are probably more effective than individual counseling for most recovering people for several reasons. First, they reinforce the common struggle, reminding you that you are neither the first nor the last to suffer from alcoholism. Second, they provide practical advice on

living without alcohol and drugs—information many therapists do not possess. Third, when confrontation is needed to penetrate denial or prevent relapse, a group is always more potent than an individual. As the saying goes, if one person says you're a horse, laugh; if five people say it, buy a saddle.

5. **The staff is expert in addictions treatment.** Pay close attention here. Just because someone has a clinical credential (medical doctor, psychiatrist, psychologist, nurse, social worker), that doesn't mean he or she has any particular skill or training in effective treatment of addictions. So look for a credential or experience in alcoholism or drug dependence. For example, if you need a physician, try using the medical director of a local treatment program or contacting the American Society of Addiction Medicine for a list of certified practitioners.

6. **The program has good aftercare.** It takes about a year for most people to stabilize sobriety. Does the program help you through the difficult initial months where you're reorganizing your life and experiencing the greatest amount of physical and psychological change? That's the purpose of aftercare.

7. **The program is oriented toward preventing relapse.** In other words, a primary goal involves teaching you how to avoid going back to alcohol or drugs. More on this in the next Chapter.

8. **The program should also provide family education and counseling.** If for no other reason that an untreated family often provokes relapse. Ask about family sessions and what is taught in them.

THE SECOND MILESTONE: STOP DRINKING
OR USING DRUGS

And we mean completely. You may have thought abstinence was the goal of treatment, but as far as we're concerned, it's the starting point, whether you believe in God or not—the baseline behavior for long-term recovery.

Drugs affect not only the way you act but also the way you think and feel, especially when you reach the point of chronic toxicity. By then, as Milam notes, you may actually suffer more (because of withdrawal and craving) in the absence of chemicals than when intoxicated. Consider yourself under the influence not only when your BAL (blood alcohol level) is high, but also when your body is struggling to cleanse itself of toxins.

So the initial goal of treatment is to pass safely through a period of withdrawal. This is not always a benign process, and we recommend it be conducted under medical supervision. Some of you may pride yourselves on going cold turkey, but there is good scientific evidence that abrupt, untreated withdrawal is bad for your system, because of excessive compensatory secretion of powerful stress hormones. So find yourself a doctor or clinic to monitor your progress. Your family physician may not have the requisite expertise, but there are probably inpatient detoxification centers in your community, as well as physicians who specialize in outpatient detoxification. Don't ignore them.

There is a common misconception that suffering severe withdrawal helps to condition the alcoholic against relapse. In our combined forty years of addictions treatment, we have met very few persons who claim to have abstained for good because of the memory of withdrawal. The brain naturally distances itself from the recollection of pain, anyway. If that weren't the case, the competitive skier who falls down a steep mountain and breaks her leg would never get up on skis again.

Avoid, however, several common errors during the detoxification phase. Some examples include: Striving for reduced consumption instead of abstinence: Many addicts enter treatment with the goal of restoring control over drugs rather than renouncing them entirely. They develop elaborate arguments to camouflage their faith in, and worship of, the "false god" of alcohol or drugs. They claim that drug use has on many occasions been a positive experience; that in the past they were able to function despite drugs; that even now, when drug use is at its worst, they are sometimes able to stop on their own. They may even cite research which supports the idea that alcoholics can return to controlled drinking.

The flaws in this reasoning are obvious. We acknowledge that drug use can be a positive experience; after all, that's why people use them. In the initial stages of the disease, drugs probably work better for the addict than for anyone else. That has no bearing on continued use. The diabetic may love chocolate bars, but must abstain from them or pay a penalty.

Second, the fact that you have historically been able to function despite your drug use is not surprising. In fact, it's characteristic of addiction, as discussed in Chapter Two. This progressive disease, however, gradually robs you of that capability. The fact that you still have periods of apparent high functioning does not obviate the increasing signs of loss of control. Look at the Figure 3-2: Note how episodes of loss of control become more severe and the periods between them—where you're functioning as you have in the past— grow ever more brief.

FIGURE 3-2

Progressive Loss of Control Over Consumption

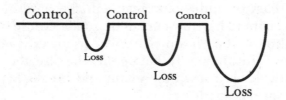

Episodes of loss of control increase in frequency and severity while periods of high function diminish.

Third, most of the research which purported to show that alcoholics could return to controlled drinking has been discredited. One study by Mark and Linda Sobell, which received considerable attention in the media, seemed to indicate that with behavior modification alcoholics could learn to drink without problems. A ten-year follow-up study of the Sobells' original group, conducted by

Mary Pendery, revealed that all but one of the "controlled drinkers" had experienced further severe problems with alcohol—in fact, several were dead of alcohol-related causes. The one "success story," by the way, had probably not been alcoholic to begin with.

Another common error involves switching from drug to drug in futile attempts to find a "safe" substance. Bedeviled by cocaine or alcohol, you substitute marijuana or a tranquilizer—your addictive thinking always leading you back to a "chemical god" as the solution to your problems.

"I never had any problem with marijuana," you think. "And the way it makes me feel is completely different from the sensation I get from drinking. Plus, I've heard it's actually less harmful physically. So when I'm tense or get a craving, I'll just smoke a joint."

If only life were that simple. Though marijuana is quite different chemically from alcohol or coke, it alters your perceptions and diminishes your resolve to avoid drinking or other drug use. And even though you can tell the difference between vodka and Valium, your body can't; that's why we use such sedative-hypnotics in detoxification programs. By displacing your faith from one drug to another, you're merely keeping yourself in a state of subservience.

The third error involves the common practice of interspersing episodes of abstinence with binges. For example, the alcoholic may follow a three-day drunk with three weeks of abstinence, proudly pointing to those days of sobriety as a sign of progress, when in fact it usually means he's getting worse. One former patient defended his behavior thusly: "In the previous fifteen years of my life, I never went a day without using some kind of mind-altering drug. Prior to this last binge, I was completely clean for nearly thirty-six days, only twelve of which were in confinement. As far as I'm concerned, that's a major achievement. You people ought to be patting me on the back instead of acting like I'm doing something wrong."

This twisted logic works only if you view abstinence as the goal of recovery, rather than the starting point. From our perspective, that's ridiculous. Alcoholics have been stopping and starting for thousands of years; most of the founding members of Alcoholics Anonymous had sworn off alcohol hundreds of times in the past, without success. The problem was *remaining* sober. That, of course, is the real goal of treatment. And it takes a kind of faith—faith in the goal of lasting sobriety—that you may have never experienced before.

THE THIRD MILESTONE: JOINING A
SELF-HELP GROUP

To understand the importance of the self-help movement in addictions, you must remember that alcoholism and drug dependence are very old illnesses. Men have consumed alcoholic beverages for approximately ten thousand years; they have cultivated cocaine, opium, and marijuana for about half that span. It requires no stretch of the imagination to believe that alcoholics and addicts have been around for nearly as long as the drugs themselves.

For most of alcohol's remarkable existence—actually, all but about sixty years of it—there existed no effective treatment. The overwhelming majority of alcoholics and addicts simply died, as a direct or indirect result of their illness. Think about the implications of that statement. We may be talking about *hundreds of millions* of lives devastated by disease. And we're not even counting the suffering of families.

Here's the amazing part: that's no longer true. Though addiction is still one of our biggest killers and the cause of untold societal misery, effective treatment does exist—as evidenced by the millions of recovering persons alive today.

Exactly how many recovering people are there? Nobody knows for sure. Alcoholics Anonymous estimates that about 1.5 million Americans attend AA meetings regularly, but that figure doesn't include those who attended meetings for a while, established stable sobriety, and no longer actively participate in AA. Dr. James Milam, author of *Under the Influence,* suggests that this is a much *larger* population than the active members. And we haven't even included those who attend meetings of Narcotics Anonymous, Cocaine Anonymous, Al-anon, Women for Sobriety, Rational Recovery, Secular Sobriety, Adult Children of Alcoholics, or who recover outside of these fellowships, on their own or through churches, clinics, and psychotherapy.

In one sense, we are witnessing a reversal of a major historical pattern. To what do we attribute this? For one, to the widespread acceptance of the disease concept, which destigmatizes alcoholism and addiction and makes recovery socially acceptable. Partly to the research which has begun to construct a model of addiction as a treatable medical condition, contradicting the longstanding prejudice of the medical community. But most of all, credit belongs to the self-help movement. For their members, such groups have often meant the difference not only between sobriety and drunkenness, but between life and death.

Obviously, the self-help movement comes in many forms, and addresses many different problems. But from the standpoint of the nonbeliever who wants to give up alcohol and drugs, it can be broken down into three principal groups.

THE TWELVE STEP PROGRAMS

In spite of their emphasis on spirituality, Twelve Step groups have from the beginning included many nonbelievers, both agnostic and atheist. In fact, it's probably safe to say there are more atheists and agnostics within AA and its related organizations than in all other self-help groups combined.

Twelve Step programs derived their foundation from the Christian self-help movements of the late nineteenth and early twentieth centuries. Two recovering alcoholics—a stockbroker named Bill Wilson and a surgeon, Bob Smith—were able to remain sober using the principles (and attending the meetings) of the Oxford Groups.

Many of the early members of AA were from Roman Catholic backgrounds, but meetings were customarily held in the Protestant churches which were more receptive to the new organization. Because many of the original members had previously failed in psychoanalysis, an early joke described AA as "a bunch of Catholic alcoholics meeting in Protestant basements to get away from Jewish psychiatrists."

The Twelve Steps themselves were derived from the Ten Principles of the Oxford Groups and subsequently left as "suggestions" for those who would follow in their footsteps. A complete discussion of the Twelve Steps from the perspective of the nonbeliever appears in Chapter Four.

Twelve Step meetings come in two principal forms: Speaker meetings, often open to the public, at which one or two members share their "experience, strength, and hope," sometimes followed by observations from the audience; and discussion meetings, usually smaller and closed to nonparticipants, centered around a topic such as one of the Steps. Speaker meetings are primarily inspirational or instructional in tone; discussion meetings are where most of the work on specific issues occurs. Though many newcomers fear speaking at meetings, direct criticism during discussion is discouraged as "taking someone else's inventory."

New members are ordinarily encouraged to attend ninety meetings in the first ninety days, both to help them bond to the organization and to structure their day during the difficult initial period of abstinence. Twelve Step groups also rely on sponsorship, a one-to-one relationship within which a more experienced member helps a newcomer to apply the Steps to his or her own recovery.

One reason for the variety of groups available (AA, Narcotics Anonymous, Cocaine Anonymous, et al) is that Twelve Step programs work on the principle of "attraction rather than promotion." They want to encourage the alcoholic or addict who still suffers to identify with the stories he or she hears at meetings. Because the experience of a cocaine or heroin addict is substantially different from that of an alcoholic, groups proliferate. In AA terms, all it takes to start a meeting is "two drunks and a coffeepot."

Some groups are highly secular, while others tend toward the religious—it all depends upon the background of the attendees. But in most areas, there's usually a large selection of AA groups to choose from, giving you the opportunity to shop around for the one you're most comfortable with. And regardless of the group's religious composition, religious worship is never the purpose of meetings. A group exists in order to maintain the sobriety of all its members. Period.

Here's an example of the value of "shopping" for the right meeting.

Marion's first contact with Alcoholics Anonymous was at age twenty-two, the result of a drunk-driving arrest. The court required her to attend at least one meeting weekly for three months. She complied, but found the meeting almost intolerable—she hated what she called the "phony piety" and the ritual recitation of the Lord's Prayer (complete with hand-holding) at the end. Naturally, she never went back after completing her sentence.

Sixteen years later, she returned—this time as a patient in an alcoholism rehab program. The program's policy was to take patients to a different meeting each night, and although the first few fit her preconception of "the same old pseudo-spiritual rigmarole," she was surprised to discover that the fourth, a women's discussion group, was virtually bereft of religious trappings. The group spent most of the meeting discussing problems adjusting to life without alcohol, and by the end of the hour, Marion felt like she'd made several new friends. She was even more surprised when the group simply broke up without the traditional recital of the Lord's Prayer. "Oh, we just dropped it," another woman informed her. "Didn't seem important anymore."

Marion made this her home group, and did not miss a meeting for eight years.

The last (or perhaps the first) cornerstone of Twelve Step philosophy is the belief in a Higher Power—a force outside the addict which can restore sanity—and indeed, this concept has proved difficult not only for atheists and agnostics but for many religious persons, as well. That's because the Steps ask you not only to believe in such a Power, but to actively turn your will and your life over to it. For nonbelievers, especially those who take pride in their relentless skepticism, the Steps will require an unfamiliar leap of faith and a categorical admission that the only real help lies outside themselves.

RATIONAL RECOVERY

Rational Recovery groups began to appear in the 1980s and like AA were founded by recovering alcoholics. From its inception, RR has rejected the spiritual orientation of the Steps and also the disease concept itself in favor of a cognitive psychological approach based on the writings of Albert Ellis, the originator of Rational Emotive

Therapy, a widely used therapy technique from the discipline of cognitive psychology. RR groups vary widely but generally differ from AA in the following respects:

1. **Attendance:** Most RR members attend only once a week, as opposed to the daily attendance schedule encouraged for newcomers to AA.

2. **Group Size:** RR has no equivalent to AA's large open speaker's meeting. The typical RR meeting more closely resembles an AA discussion group in size and tone. Meetings are generally limited to no more than twelve participants.

3. **Use of the term "alcoholic":** Most RR members avoid the label of alcoholic. Many believe that calling oneself an alcoholic externalizes the decision-making process and relieves one of the responsibility for choosing to drink or not to drink.

4. **Alcoholism as a disease:** Although the AA literature is not based on a disease concept, most AA members subscribe to the view that alcoholism is in fact a disease. RR members do not. They believe (along the lines described by Albert Ellis) that problem drinkers make incorrect or shortsighted choices based on emotional states. RR members often refer to their desire to drink as "The Beast" within themselves.

5. **Duration of membership:** Where AA members may continue to attend indefinitely (and many do), RR members usually stop attending after about six to ten months in the group. They sometimes go back to deal with specific crises or if relapse occurs.

6. **The Higher Power:** RR members do not believe a higher power is necessary for recovery, instead emphasizing understanding of psychological issues and a return of self-control.

The existence of Rational Recovery is evidence that this approach works for many. After all, the Rational Emotive Therapy techniques of Albert Ellis (upon which RR is based) are used by many treatment programs, including ours. But there remains a hidden flaw, perhaps not only with the RR model but with the entire *psychogenic paradigm* from which it springs. Ultimately, alcoholism and addiction cannot be fully understood as purely psychological phenomena. An approach which relies exclusively on identifying and resolving "underlying issues" and on reasserting self-control is, in our experience, doomed to failure with the great majority of addicts and alcoholics.

So our advice: If RR meetings alone don't get the result you seek, supplement them with something else.

THE SECULAR SOBRIETY GROUPS

Secular Sobriety was founded by James Christopher, a recovering alcoholic in Alcoholics Anonymous who left the organization because of his objection to spiritual content of the Steps and the continued insistence on use of a Higher Power. In his 1988 book, *How to Stay Sober: Recovery Without Religion,* Christopher describes himself as a "freethinker" who believes that sobriety is best achieved through an emphasis on self-reliance and self-knowledge. Secular Sobriety meetings often resemble AA discussion groups; most sessions feature a sobriety-related topic, and there is considerable emphasis on practicing a daily program of recovery and remaining abstinent no matter what the provocation to drink. For example, Christopher suggests that each Secular Sobriety member keep a weekly journal, wherein he or she records the following each day: "My name is _____ and I am a ____. I do not ____ *no matter what.* I prioritize my ____ above all else." (*How to Stay Sober*, Prometheus Books, 1988, p.131)

Christopher also makes extensive use of slogans, such as "Today is all we have. I won't drink it away" and "Today I breathe the fresh air of my sobriety." In fact, much of the advice Christopher gives in his book is similar to, and sometimes appropriated from, the folk wisdom heard at AA meetings. But as a "freethinker" or secular humanist, unable to reconcile himself to the idea of a Higher Power, Christopher chose to develop the Secular Sobriety alternative. He maintains that the secular approach develops increased self-esteem instead of promoting unhealthy dependence upon a "mythical" power greater than oneself.

Unlike RR, these meetings are devoted to the idea that alcoholism is a chronic and progressive disease and that the alcoholic is unable to drink because of a physiological rather than a psychological abnormality. Christopher explains craving as a simple Pavlovian response resulting from years of turning to alcohol or drugs in response to nearly any stress. In this respect, Christopher's philosophy is probably more closely tied to the disease model than is that of many Twelve Step groups.

One additional area where Secular Sobriety groups differ from Twelve Step fellowships is in their approach to sponsorship. Christopher relates several stories of bad advice he received from his sponsors in AA, and as a result Secular Sobriety avoids sponsorship, preferring that members relate to one another on an equal footing.

CHOOSING AMONG THE SELF-HELP GROUPS

From the nonbeliever's standpoint, the most important difference between the three organizations is simple availability—not religion. There are tens of thousands of Twelve Step meetings, and if you live in an urban area you can probably choose among several on any given night of the week. There are fewer Secular Sobriety Groups although they proliferate easily and Christopher describes the procedures for starting a meeting in his book. Rational Recovery meetings are still less common. Since they limit group size and frequency of attendance and members usually stay only six months, RR's focus is far more limited. In our area, there are currently six groups meeting on different nights of the week. With an average attendance of twelve per group, that implies an active membership of seventy-two people.

That isn't much in the way of support. For every addict who is able to successfully remain abstinent attending one meeting weekly, we can identify two or three more who will experience repeated relapses. If you choose to attend RR or Secular Sobriety meetings, we suggest supplementing them with attendance at the appropriate

Twelve Step group until your sobriety is well established. Even if you object to the Higher Power, there are still a lot of practical benefits to be derived from the company of other recovering persons. But you have to be willing to give yourself over to the power of collaboration. You have to allow yourself to break out of the isolating skepticism and arrogance long enough to at least sample the strength that can be found in a community of recovering addicts.

And remember, the larger goal is to stay sober, by whatever means.

THE FOURTH MILESTONE: LEARNING ABOUT YOUR DISEASE

You may believe you know a great deal about alcoholism or drug addiction when you enter treatment, but all your experience is in the realm of being sick. You may know little or nothing about how to recover.

Above all else, you need accurate information about your illness. Because we have no cure for alcoholism or addiction, treatment doesn't remove the disease. It simply teaches you how to live with it. The behavior and attitude change which constitutes recovery is your responsibility.

That's analogous to the dilemma faced by the diabetic or the heart patient. To have a chance at survival, you must learn to take on many of the responsibilities you normally turn over to the physician. Your doctors, nurses, and counselors become consultants to the primary caregiver—*you*. Ultimate success or failure—or if you will, life or death—is dependent upon your willingness to cooperate.

Whether you believe in God or not, the facts about your disease are always going to be the same. The disease of addiction will affect the body of a nonbeliever in exactly the same way it would affect that of the most religious zealot who ever lived.

Thus, we recommend you become an expert in the treatment of addiction. Learn everything you can about it. First, learn something about the disease itself. Read this book cover to cover. Explore the texts listed in the back of the book. Research the philosophy and approach of the various self-help fellowships. You can start with AA-oriented literature or with the alternatives offered by Secular Sobriety or Rational Recovery, but no matter which you prefer, you should learn something about *all* the options. Feel free to read anything else that strikes your interest. When you're done, you should have a decent background in the disease which is affecting your life.

You should be able to define the following terms:

Tolerance
Withdrawal
Craving
Compulsion
Loss of Control
Continued use despite adverse consequences
Blackout
Enabling
Codependency
Maintenance pattern
Detoxification
Sponsor

In fact, why don't you write these terms on a piece of paper and put it by the chair where you do most of your reading. As you come across the various explanations of the above terms, jot them down. You're assembling a glossary for future use—so when people use these words, you can interpret them accurately.

You may find that the best way to check the clarity of your understanding of these terms is to teach them to someone else. If you can explain them clearly and answer questions about their meaning, you understand them.

THE FIFTH MILESTONE: BEGIN LOOKING AT YOUR PROBLEMS FROM A BIOGENIC PERSPECTIVE

James Milam uses the term *biogenic* to mean caused by or resulting from biological activity. It is the opposite of *psychogenic*, which refers to causation by psychological factors. Milam makes the point—with which we wholeheartedly agree—that nearly every important aspect of addictive disease can be explained without resorting to speculation about motive or psychology. And this makes it easier to think of addiction as a disease rather than a moral or psychological problem—a much more solid basis for recovery.

For example, suppose last year you gave up drinking in an effort to please your family. But to everyone's surprise, you discovered that you're even more unhappy and depressed sober than when drinking. Even your loved ones commented on how unpleasant you were. After a month or so of conflict, you finally gave up and returned to alcohol. "Maybe I'm one of those people who just *need* it, psychologically," you conclude. "I couldn't relax, I couldn't sleep, I was always on edge." Your family concurs. "It sounds terrible," your wife admits, "but he was actually nicer when he was drinking. Maybe he can't quit. Maybe he just has an addictive personality."

That's a classic example of destructive psychogenic interpretation. The underlying assumption made by both parties is that when alcohol is removed, the alcoholic should immediately begin to function better. When discomfort persists, they take that as a sign that something else is wrong—some mysterious emotional disorder, no doubt, which secretly underlies the alcoholism. If you read Chapter Six, however, you'll learn that because the alcoholic's body has become dependent on alcohol, cessation of drinking is followed by a period of withdrawal, characterized by irritability, insomnia, and anxiety. Though the acute phase lasts only a week or so, the protracted withdrawal syndrome may wax and wane for months. In light of this, your experience of persistent discomfort was typical of alcoholics who stop on their own. But where a psychogenic interpretation of this experience led you and your family to believe that you would never feel comfortable without alcohol, a biogenic view might have encouraged you to continue with abstinence long enough for the symptoms to abate.

It's a crucial difference, isn't it? You might not have believed that perspective could be so important. But it's a bit like those illustrations of figure and ground used in art and psychology classes. What appears to be the silhouette of a beautiful young woman can, when viewed differently, reveal the unmistakable profile of a hideous crone. It's all in where you look.

The biogenic perspective is far easier for the newly sober person to understand and use as a foundation for recovery. It's simple, straightforward, and motivates people toward productive change. Unfortunately, it's not the perspective we're taught as children. Most of us grew up believing that alcoholics and addicts were people with underlying moral and psychological problems whose injured psyches would probably never permit them to live without alcohol and drugs. Many of us were taught that the only way out was through an act of God (it's no wonder the original members of AA relied so heavily on spiritual conversion). But recovery from disease is not contingent upon a "born again" conversion.

This heavy psychogenic programming means that the recovering person must often undergo what Milam calls a "paradigm shift" to a biogenic view—a process which produces a lot of cognitive dissonance. In other words, much of what you learn in the early phases of treatment will be at odds with your previous views, causing you to feel uncomfortable with it. You, as a nonbeliever, proud of your self-sufficiency, will probably be most resistant to the idea of having to look outside yourself for help. "That can't be the case," you'll think. "It's more self-control I need—not less." It's a wrenching process.

The biogenic versus psychogenic conflict exists throughout the field of addiction treatment. Psychiatry has also experienced it. American psychiatrists by and large followed the path of Freud and the psychoanalysts, articulating a psychology based on early childhood experience and a reliance on "talk therapy." By contrast, psychiatrists in Europe stayed true to the principles of medicine, defined common psychiatric disorders in terms of symptoms and probable causes, and concentrated on developing biological treatments. As it has become more and more apparent that schizophrenia, bipolar disorder, and depression are more effectively treated with medication than psychoanalysis, the biogenic view has superseded that of Freud.

We're not saying that psychological factors play no role in addiction. We're simply saying that most of what you experience as an addict or alcoholic can be explained without resorting to complex, often confusing theories about the impact of childhood on adult behavior. As you read the literature about alcoholism, strive to see yourself as physiologically rather than psychologically ill. Remember that the treatment of the disease has little to do with a search for God or the cleansing of moral weakness. Search for actions you can take to bring yourself back in line with the "wisdom of the body."

BEGINNING YOUR PARADIGM SHIFT

Here's an exercise you can try to facilitate the transition from a psychogenic to a biogenic perspective. Write out a history of your experience with alcohol and drugs. Divide it into five-year blocks. For example, if you're thirty-six years old now, and began drinking when you were fifteen, divide it under subheadings like: The First Five Years (ages 15 through 19); the Second Five Years (ages 20 through 24); and so on. Now, using your earlier reading as a guide, reinterpret your experience in terms of your understanding of a chronic, physiological disease. In other words, identify the symptoms of addiction in your experience (once again, refer to the appropriate Bell Chart in the Appendix for your primary drug). Wherever you feel that something was truly caused by psychological problems, try re-explaining it in terms of underlying biology.

For example, suppose when you were seventeen you made an abortive suicide attempt. In the past, you might have explained that in terms of depression over the loss of a girlfriend or boyfriend. But was there also a biogenic component? In other words, did your drug or alcohol use influence in any way your desire to hurt yourself? Were you under the influence (or in withdrawal) when you made the attempt? Had you been drinking or using drugs in the days or weeks prior to trying to kill yourself, which contributed heavily to your depression? Did your alcohol or drug use play a role in the breakup or deterioration of the relationship itself? Is there a history of depression or alcoholism in your family, which might indicate a predisposition to this type of behavior?

We're not denying the importance of psychology; instead, we're emphasizing the key role of biology. The science of psychopharmacology (the study of psychoactive drugs) is based on the assumption that everything we think, feel, or do corresponds to activity on a biological substrate. Since we *define* the alcoholic and addict by the way in which he or she consumes powerful, mood-changing chemicals, it would be indefensible to deny the overwhelming importance of these chemical processes in explaining subsequent behavior. Don't make that error yourself.

THE SIXTH MILESTONE: SELF-DIAGNOSIS

Now that you've taken the information you have learned and applied it to your own experience, identifying symptoms of addiction as they have presented themselves, you're ready to arrive at the conclusion that you suffer from a chronic, progressive, addictive disease. That's called self-diagnosis.

Of all the things that happen in treatment, self-diagnosis is the most important. That's because it's the source of your motivation for continued sobriety.

Let's clarify that. Addicts and alcoholics initially enter treatment for one or more of many different reasons. Perhaps your job is in jeopardy, or your spouse has threatened divorce. Maybe you've been severely depressed, even thinking about suicide. You're sick and tired of feeling physically sick and tired, or worrying about where your next hit is coming from. Maybe the judge has ordered you to get help, or you'll lose your driver's license.

Whatever the reason, it's fairly short term. In a matter of weeks or months, the crisis that spurred your cry for assistance will abate, and eventually disappear. That's because time heals all wounds, especially when you're no longer bathing your brain in toxins or making the kind of stupid, ill-timed decisions that people make in the throes of intoxication and withdrawal.

When the crisis goes, so will your motivation for sobriety. "After all," you think, "I'm doing okay. Where's the harm in a couple of drinks, socially? What's wrong with one joint? If I was in a jam I wouldn't dream of it, but now that things are going good, why not?"

You reintroduce the chemical, your disease is reactivated, and before you know it, you're back in trouble—often worse than the last episode—and kicking yourself for having blown a good thing.

In fact, many later-stage alcoholics and addicts live from crisis to crisis. When they're in hot water, they're on the phone begging for assistance or running to doctors and counselors or borrowing money which they have every intention of repaying, when they're back on their feet again. As soon as the crisis is resolved, they slip right back into their old behavior.

This might be diagrammed as follows:

denial   denial   denial

    crisis   .   crisis   crisis (cry for help)

Crisis periods are windows in denial which can lead to much-needed treatment. Still, the incentive which drives you to seek help is not always the same one which ultimately keeps you sober. The first type (which we'll call *short-term* motivation) is almost always: 1. **external:** a response, sometimes quite impulsive, to an outside stress or difficulty which the addict perceives as beyond his capacity to address without assistance from others; 2. **transient:** the result of a confluence of circumstances which by its very nature may disappear over a few weeks or months; and 3. **noninsightful:** that is, the alcoholic seeks treatment as a way to avoid or relieve suffering but doesn't see the role of addiction in precipitating the crisis, or may in fact believe that alcohol or drug use has little or nothing to do with it.

That's one of the reasons forced treatment (for example, by the courts) or family intervention (organized efforts by family members to get someone into treatment) ultimately have about the same success rate as voluntary admission. People frequently ask us if treatment can work unless the alcoholic really "wants" to get sober. But of course, a newly sober alcoholic is ambivalent about sobriety. On the one hand, she recalls the years when alcohol was both best friend and sole comfort. On the other, she currently suffers problems brought about by drinking. She enters treatment because problems temporarily outweigh rewards. When that changes, so will her attitude.

Never underestimate the addict's inability to perceive the causative role of drugs in his own difficulties. One former patient has been arrested three times in three years for drug possession and sales. We asked him what he thought that meant. "I'm unlucky," he asserted.

And when interviewed further, he provided a separate rationalization for each arrest. "In 1987, I was turned in by somebody else because they were trying to get off on another charge," he insisted. "In eighty-eight, I just happened to be crashin' in this apartment which the cops busted by mistake—they were lookin' for the place next door, but they saw drugs and arrested us anyway. That was cold. Then in eighty-nine, this bitch I used to hang with set me up. So you can see, I'm really like a victim here."

By his lights, the problem isn't that he uses and sells drugs but that he gets arrested. He arrives in detox not to recover from heroin addiction but to avoid a jail sentence and (he hopes) to learn how to stay away from the police. It's easy to see that he will relapse shortly after leaving the hospital—an observation which he bitterly disputes. "You people are always so negative," he tells the other group members. "How do you know I won't stay clean this time? Show me your crystal ball. I know myself, and I know I'm right." Obstinate as ever, he insists he can take care of his own problems. Regardless of his feelings about religion and faith, his stubbornness blinds him to the fact that drugs have become his false god—one his disease forces him to worship.

The next time he shows up in detox—a few months later—he has another excuse. "I was doin' fine, but a couple days after I left here this guy showed up at my door and laid a bunch of dope on me. What am I supposed to do, turn it down? I'm an addict."

That's also why counselors normally ignore an alcoholic's protestations that he's learned his lesson and will never drink again. Recovery from addictive disease isn't a matter of learning your lesson. It's a matter of examining your experience, drawing the appropriate conclusions, becoming motivated for change, and then making those changes in the way you think and act. It's also a matter of faith—faith in the support and guidance of others, faith in your own ability to recover. Promises mean nothing.

The second type of motivation, which we'll call *long term*, is characterized by the following features.

1. It's **internalized:** that is, based on a healthy fear of the possible consequences of continued drinking or drug use;

2. It's **lasting,** because it doesn't spring from a crisis; and

3. It's **insightful,** stemming from understanding of the illness and its role in bringing about your current and past difficulties.

This is what keeps you sober. It doesn't happen overnight. The best way to achieve long-term motivation is through a process of self-diagnosis, which should occur during treatment. Your incentive to stay sober, therefore, should increase as a result of the treatment process.

How to Self-Diagnose

As you went through your drinking and drug history, you may have found yourself rejecting the idea that you have alcoholism or addiction. Perhaps you remain in doubt, because of a number of objections that persist in your thinking. That's quite common. But you can't overcome these objections by yourself, because if you are indeed addicted, your many unconscious defenses will interfere with recognition of symptoms.

Let's briefly review how these defenses interfere with self-diagnosis.

Denial is an inability to perceive a problem despite evidence one exists. Let's watch as Bill, a fifty-four-year-old attorney, defends his behavior at last night's party to his wife, in spite of the fact that he doesn't recall much of the evening:

BILL: Sure, I drank too much, I never made a pass at anybody's daughter. What do you take me for? You're accepting her word against mine?

WIFE: But why would she lie? She was nearly hysterical.

BILL: How the hell would I know? Maybe it's her period. Am I supposed to understand the mind of a twenty-year-old?

WIFE: I'm scared, Bill. This isn't the first time . . . maybe you need Alcoholics Anonymous . . .

BILL: So now I'm not only a dirty old man, I'm a wino who needs
  to find God?

WIFE: I'm not even sure you remember last night. You were so
  drunk.

BILL: Oh, that's just terrific. Now I not only have to defend my
  good name against everybody else, but against you, too . . .

We know that Bill doesn't recall what he said or did, so he's basing
his defense entirely on his belief that his character would never
permit him to do something immoral. But that's not the real focus
of his anxiety: Bill had a blackout, and doesn't want his wife to find
out. Why not? Because people who have blackouts are alcoholics. If
he can keep this symptom hidden, he can explain it away later.
"Everybody forgets from time to time," he'll tell himself. "I'll watch
my drinking in the future."

To self-diagnose, Bill must admit the possibility of such behavior
during blackout periods—not because it "fits" with this self-image,
or has anything to do with morality, but because it is consistent with
the disease.

Rationalization involves providing alternative reasons for alcohol or
drug-related problems. Here's Elizabeth, whose mother arrived at
her apartment an hour ago to find her daughter unconscious on the
couch.

ELIZABETH: I did not pass out. I fell asleep. That bottle of wine
  was nearly empty when I got it out of the refrigerator. I only
  had one or two glasses.

MOTHER: I could not rouse you. It took me fifteen minutes to
  wake you up. That didn't happen on one or two glasses of
  wine.

ELIZABETH: The reason you couldn't rouse me was because of
  the antihistamine I'm taking. I guess the interaction with the
  wine was too much for my system.

MOTHER: I don't know. That sounds awfully convenient. Besides,
  I've seen you take antihistamines all your life, and this never
  happened. And you reek of alcohol.

ELIZABETH: I'm surprised that you don't trust your own flesh and blood, mother. You're always looking for the worst in everyone.

Elizabeth is reaching for any alternative explanation to account for the fact that she drank to unconsciousness. When her mother counters her excuses, Elizabeth goes on the offensive, accusing her of mistrust. To self-diagnose, Elizabeth must abandon such complicated rationalizations in favor of a simpler, more obvious observation: She has a drinking problem.

Externalizing means blaming your behavior on outside forces or circumstances. Les, a rock drummer, describes the reason he uses drugs to his counselor:

LES: It's around all the time, you know? Drugs and rock go together, always have, always will. I don't wanna use the stuff, but what are you going to do? You're on the road all the time, away from home, in hotel rooms, fooling around with groupies, and somebody always has some blow.
COUNSELOR: What about all the musicians that have given up drugs?
LES: Hey, man, most of them nearly died before they did. They were real burnouts, you know? Plus, I bet most of them are chipping around. I heard one guy was back in detox.
COUNSELOR: Sounds like you're in a no-win situation.
LES: I wish I could quit, to be honest. But the music's in my blood, man.

Note how Les undermines the counselor's suggestion that other musicians have learned to live without drugs. If someone else can recover, it implies that Les could, as well—something he doesn't want to acknowledge. To self-diagnose, Les must acknowledge the possibility of sobriety.

Minimizing involves discounting the importance of alcohol- or drug-related problems, thus obviating the need for action. James, a forty-year-old businessman, responds to a friend who has confronted him about a drinking episode:

> James: Look, other people drink too much on occasion. I've seen them. I've even seen you with a couple under your belt. Remember that time Phil got so drunk I had to drive him home? Nobody criticized him. Yet I have a couple too many one night and everybody gets on my case.
>
> Friend: More than once, Jamie. More like once a month.
>
> James: Okay, a few nights, but you have to admit that most of the time I function very well.
>
> Friend: I'm not saying you don't. But every once in a while, you really go overboard.
>
> James: Hey, you know what, you're right. You've really opened my eyes. I'm gonna cut back, make sure that never happens again. You're a real pal, you know that?

James assumes that now that he knows better, he'll be able to change his behavior. His own experience contradicts this: Sooner or later, he'll revert to his old patterns. But he convinces himself that his most recent resolutions will be successful where past efforts haven't been. In order to self-diagnose, he will have to acknowledge his own history of failed promises and the likelihood that such vows are not the answer.

Intellectualizing is an overemphasis on insignificant or irrelevant issues in order to avoid a larger, anxiety-provoking question (such as whether or not you have alcoholism). Here's Biff, thirty-nine, a street drug addict, upset upon first learning that his life expectancy is not as long as he had hoped:

> Biff: When you say the average life span of an addict is fifty years, is that the mean, the median, or the mathematical average?
>
> Doctor: It's the average age of people who die of drug-related causes.
>
> Biff: Yeah, but what is the methodology used to determine that?
>
> Doctor: They look at death certificates, I suppose.

BIFF: Yeah, but does that include just people who died of over-
doses, or victims of homicide, or people who intentionally kill
themselves, like with guns?

DOCTOR: I'd have to look it up. I don't think they said in the
article.

BIFF: Well, you better be sure, because I don't think you could
include suicides, because what if it was because they found out
they had AIDS or something? You'd have to include that in the
AIDS statistics, even though it wasn't actually AIDS that killed
them. So I think you should do more research before you go
spreading that kind of thing around and upsetting people.

DOCTOR: Are you sure this is really important?

BIFF: Hey, you said it, not me. Just want to make sure you got
your facts straight. Besides, I knew a junkie once who had to be
seventy years old. At least, he sure looked it.

The doctor's discussion of shortened life spans makes Biff nervous, so he questions its validity. Skepticism is healthy, but Biff isn't
really interested in the scientific methodology; he's more than willing to reject the research in favor of stories about "a junkie" he once
knew. He's simply undermining the validity of the evidence, not
unlike a lawyer trying to get his client off on a technicality. Perhaps
he'll succeed. But like the attorney who wins his client's freedom
only to discover he robs and kills again, Biff will find that simply
rejecting evidence is not enough. What happens when he returns to
drug use? The ultimate judge is still waiting.

To self-diagnose, Biff must stop sabotaging information about
the disease and develop a plan to treat it.

Then there's the age-old problem of *comparing out*. You find
yourself concentrating on the symptoms you don't have rather than
the ones you do, as though the absence of a given symptom freed
you from the diagnosis. Here's Ted with his counselor:

TED: Blackouts? Hey, I never had a blackout. Maybe I'm not
alcoholic after all. Or at least not very far advanced.

COUNSELOR: Only about fifty percent of alcoholics have blackouts. The rest don't. Let's move on to see if you have any other
symptoms.

TED: Wait a minute. If I haven't had a blackout, does that mean I'm statistically less likely to be alcoholic at all?

COUNSELOR: I don't understand the question.

TED: I just want to know if the rate of alcoholism in the group that has the blackouts is higher than the group that doesn't. It seems like it would be, doesn't it?

COUNSELOR: Even if it was, it wouldn't mean you weren't alcoholic yourself. You have many other symptoms.

TED: But it would mean it was less likely, wouldn't it?

See the lengths to which Ted must go in order to reject the diagnosis of addiction? He's frightened of being an alcoholic, because of the obligation for abstinence that accompanies recognition of the disease. That's why it's so comical when critics of the disease concept argue that it relieves the alcoholic of responsibility for his drinking. If it did, more would be willing to self-diagnose. Because it doesn't, addicts resist the diagnosis. This is especially true for nonbelievers. As we've seen in previous illustrations, that old and all-encompassing skepticism makes it even harder to self-diagnose, despite the presence of cold, clinical facts.

Although most alcoholics and addicts have partially self-diagnosed before entering treatment, the true, complete self-diagnosis which forms the basis of long-term motivation and sobriety usually comes as a result of the treatment process itself. Time, too, plays a role. As the weeks and months pass, your brain, cleansed of toxins, recalls more and more of the past. In treatment, you may consider your drinking problems only a couple of years old; by the end of your first year of abstinence, you may be able to point to symptoms of alcoholism which appeared in the first months of your contact with alcohol. Your perspective is actually improving with distance.

So in the matter of self-diagnosis, your own perceptions are not as reliable as you would like. Seek outside assistance and take your time. Proceed as follows:

1. With the list of symptoms, review your history. Note any symptoms you have experienced. Write down examples of each.

2. Discuss your list with the counselor.
3. Write out a statement explaining how you came to the conclusion that you suffer from a chronic, progressive disease.
4. Write a statement describing what you plan to do to treat it.
5. Discuss this with your counselor and at least one other person who is knowledgeable about addiction. Get their feedback.

THE SEVENTH MILESTONE: LEARN TO LIVE ONE DAY AT A TIME

Sounds easy, right? It isn't. It's one of the most difficult things you will learn to do.

Most human beings explain their behavior in terms of past influences and believe they can correct it by making elaborate future plans. There isn't much basis for either practice.

Suppose when visiting a woman's house we compliment her on how neat it is. "Well, my mother was very neat," our host responds. "We were taught to pick up after ourselves."

A simple, convenient explanation. Except that the host's brothers and sisters are slobs. What happened to them? We have to come up with an explanation for their behavior, as well.

Then we happen to visit someone else whose house is even neater than hers. "Our house when we were kids was very messy," this new host says. "I guess I just reacted to that."

Two days later, another neat freak confesses she has absolutely no idea why she's so orderly. "Nobody else in my family is like that," she admits. "They're just average."

So we have several different explanations (or two explanations and one non-explanation) for the same behavior. If you're a skeptic, it will probably occur to you that perhaps none of these explains the behavior in question. Ultimately, the only thing we can be sure of is that all three people keep their houses neat because they like it that way. The rest is speculation.

Nevertheless, none of the women attributed her neatness to simple preference. Each reached into the past in an attempt to account for present behavior. It's a powerful reflex.

So is the impulse to fantasize about the future. *What will I be doing three years from now?* we wonder. Businesses hire expensive consultants to do five- and ten-year projections, most of which turn out wrong. Sports magazines prognosticate the outcome of seasons yet to be played, by players yet to be selected. People pay to have their horoscopes cast months or years in advance. Nancy Reagan allegedly used her husband's horoscope to determine his schedule (some were appalled, but we were at least happy to see that *some* system was being used). Men and women do this not because there is any reliable way to predict specific occurrences of the future, but because we wish there was. And our need is strong enough that it overwhelms our better judgment.

The normal human tendency to dwell on the past and future instead of the present is destructive to the newly sober alcoholic, however, for two reasons.

First, your past is probably strewn with difficult memories that are like land mines of resentment or remorse. As a nonbeliever, you can't really sin, because such an act would imply an offense against God's laws. But an awareness of the difference between right and wrong is not contingent upon belief in God. For the nonbeliever who is already wary of Twelve Step groups, the overwhelming nature of guilt can trigger even more skepticism—a defense that lets you run from the danger of confronting past wrongs. In your emotionally augmented condition, investigation of painful occurrences or childhood trauma will probably produce a fit of anger or depression instead of the catharsis and emotional release you seek. So wait until your nervous system is a bit steadier before digging in the closets of your psyche. Besides, you can't change any of it, can you? The most you can hope for is understanding and acceptance. And the opportunity for that doesn't go away.

Second, if you're like most newly sober people, your future is fraught with uncertainty. You don't really know what it holds. So what is the point of building castles in the air, only to watch them washed away by the tides of time? Most of the things you're afraid of won't come to pass, and most of the things you dream about now will be replaced by new dreams and aspirations.

So when you find your brain straying to the dim past or the

fantastic future, bring yourself back to the present. Let go of the guilt stemming from "sins." Rid yourself of the burden of the past and future; it restricts your recovery and keeps you from self-diagnosis. The real changes in behavior that determine whether you survive addiction occur entirely on a day-to-day basis. You really don't need the future and the past as much as you think you do.

THE EIGHTH MILESTONE: REBUILD YOUR LIFE AROUND RECOVERY

You may not have noticed the extent to which addiction has affected the rest of your life. In fact, you might look at life as proceeding smoothly except for your drug use. "If I could just get this alcohol thing under control," you think, "I'd be in good shape."

It's a bit more complicated than that. Alcohol and drugs have penetrated your existence more than you know. If you're like most addicts, drug use may actually have become what a psychologist might call the *central organizing principle* of your life.

That's an imposing term with a very straightforward meaning. It implies that not only have alcohol and drugs influenced your life-style, but much of your life has been built around drug and alcohol use. Structured so as to permit you to drink or use drugs with minimal problems. If alcohol and drugs are such a powerful component of your life, how can you possibly give up your faith in drinking or using and replace it with faith in recovery?

Here's an example of alcohol's pervasive presence.

Don, the son of an alcoholic attorney, began drinking when he was fourteen. By his second year in college, he was already a functioning alcoholic. His tolerance was high enough that he seldom looked drunk, but his need for alcohol was such that hardly a day went by when he didn't drink. Of course, he naturally gravitated toward others with similar practices, and joined the heaviest drinking fraternity on campus. In the general atmosphere of revelry, Don's consumption went unnoticed. He dated a succession of "party girls" before finally meeting his eventual wife, a nondrinking preacher's daughter from Nebraska who was studying social work at the university. That in itself isn't surprising—many early-stage alcoholics marry nondrinkers from religious backgrounds which emphasize "helping" others. Their naivete makes them perfect candidates for the syndrome of codependency and a lifetime of failed attempts to change the alcoholic.

Don's original career choice had been the law, but his poor study habits and fondness for alcohol prevented him from having a realistic chance at law school. Searching for an alternative in his senior year, he fell into a part-time job as evening manager of a singles bar in town. He seemed a natural for the position: dependable, adept at handling customers and employees, bright and even-tempered. After graduation he accepted a full-time job at a salary considerably higher than most of his fellow graduates. A year later he and Gretchen married and a year after that had their first child.

Don had received his first DWI in college and his second and third by age twenty-five. His license suspended, Don developed an ingenious system of rides to and from work, relying on his wife and various employees. With the high turnover in the bar business, Don found himself actually asking prospective waiters and bartenders whether or not they could give him a ride.

By age thirty-three, Don's alcohol consumption was the equivalent of a quart bottle of whiskey daily. He awoke at eleven A.M. had his first drink (only beer, he noted) shortly after noon, went to work at three P.M., drank with the customers (part of the job, he said) and from the bottle in his office (always from a cup, never directly from the bottle) until it was time to go home, at about one A.M. On occasion, his staff would have to help him to the car. His wife and kids were asleep when he got home, so he usually stayed up until three or four in the morning, swigging vodka (a "nightcap") until passing out on the couch or floor. His wife, angry about his drinking, took the children and moved out, filing for divorce.

At thirty-four, Don was fired from his job for excessive drinking and went on a four-month binge, after which he was admitted to the hospital for detoxification. Questioned by the counselor, Don insisted his problems with alcohol had begun about a year ago, when he and his wife had separated. "I was so lonely, so depressed," he wept. "That really put me over the top."

You can see from Don's history, however, that this was not the case. Alcoholism has dominated his life since his early teens. At first, his high tolerance seemed to be an advantage. But most of his key decisions were already being influenced by his need to accommodate his developing alcoholism. Some examples:

1. Don selected his college friends and fraternity on the basis of their drinking practices.
2. He also chose his girlfriends from the ranks of heavy drinkers and/or codependents.
3. He selected a profession where his drinking would be accommodated.
4. By the same token, drinking discouraged his dream of practicing law.
5. Afraid of drunk-driving arrests, he devised an intricate system of rides from his employees.
6. He lost his marriage because of his drinking.

Remarkable, isn't it? Don dates his alcoholism from the breakup of his marriage, when in reality the disease has at first influenced and then virtually controlled his life for nearly twenty years. Unbeknownst to Don, he has in effect *built his life around his addiction.* That same lifestyle supports and reinforces drinking, and will undermine his sobriety.

You can't just remove one key aspect and expect everything else to remain the same. Imagine a football game without the quarterback position. Who do you snap the ball to? Pretty soon, one of the other players has to shift over to play quarterback, because the game requires one. That's analogous to Don's life without alcohol. If he keeps doing things exactly the way he's always done them, he'll eventually return to drinking. It's the "engine" which drives that lifestyle. Don needs to find enough courage and faith in recovery to find a new engine for his life. Some turn to God, others don't have that option. But whether you believe in God or not, all addicts have two things in common: the disease, and the need to change the beliefs and behaviors that support it.

So look carefully at your daily routine, and how you might alter it to support sobriety rather than relapse. We recommend the following procedure:

Step 1: Each day, make a list of priorities for that day. Put "staying sober (or clean)" at the top.

Step 2: Make sure you don't replace recovery activities with tasks you convince yourself are "more important" because of some short-term goal.

Step 3: Go over your priorities with your counselor or a knowledgeable member of your self-help group. Get their feedback.

THE NINTH MILESTONE: STAY SOBER
NO MATTER WHAT

James Christopher makes a particular point of this in his book, and we couldn't agree more. The best sobriety is that which you maintain *independent* of circumstances.

In our earlier book for families, *Freeing Someone You Love from Alcohol and Other Drugs*, we noted that when an alcoholic or addict decides to abstain, he or she ordinarily builds in a number of "escape clauses"—situations in which the right to drink is reserved. The common statement, "I'm never going to drink again," should often read, "I'm never going to drink again, *unless . . .*

I lose my job
I have trouble with my spouse
I'm going to jail anyway
Somebody criticizes me
I can't sleep
I get depressed
I can't stop thinking about it
Somebody offers it to me
Something terrible happens
I'm angry about something
I have a panic attack
I'm unhappy"

and so forth. Such conditions are usually unspoken. The flaw is that sooner or later one or more of the above inevitably comes to pass, and you'll get drunk again.

And you have our sympathy. These are painful situations, and we understand how common it is for people to use alcohol to relieve the stress associated with them. As far as we're concerned, you are 100 percent justified in turning to drugs when you can't sleep, or somebody treats you unfairly, or something awful happens that wasn't your fault. We're on your side. Life can be hell.

If only your disease were as understanding as we are.

Alcoholism, of course, can't tell the difference between a good and a bad motive. Your liver and brain respond the same way to drugs consumed after a tragedy as they do to those ingested during a Christmas party. The difference may be important to you, but your body could care less. If you use too much cocaine, you will overdose. If your liver becomes inflamed, you will wind up in the hospital. If you use a dirty needle, you will become HIV positive. If you ram your car headlong into a tree, you will spend the rest of your days in a wheelchair. If you drunkenly allow your cigarette to fall in your lap, you will go up in flames. We suppose you could call it a law of nature.

Christopher recommends that you begin every day with the assertion that you will remain sober *no matter what*. Maybe paste it on your refrigerator door. Not a bad idea.

THE TENTH MILESTONE: TELL KEY PEOPLE ABOUT YOUR RECOVERY

Here's where a lot of newly sober people go wrong. They take the position that sobriety is nobody's business but their own, and exclude even their family and friends from the recovery process. In nonbelievers, this is often a manifestation of that old skepticism— that no one else could possibly understand what I've been through. This approach creates no end of conflict, and often results in an isolated addict. But by voicing your plans and ideas, you begin to give yourself a sense of community—which, you will find, is one of the greatest assets of Twelve Step groups. Remember, all it takes to form a group is "two drunks and a coffee pot."

Why else should you make a deliberate attempt to tell those around you about your recovery? People are depending on you. Just as you count on them in any number of ways, so, too, do they depend on you. If your lifestyle is about to change in substantial ways (and we hope it is), why not let them know in advance? For example, if you're going to spend the next ninety evenings at AA or Secular Sobriety meetings, sit down and explain that to them. It's just possible they don't understand why you're doing this.

"The counselors told me if he stopped drinking he'd be closer to his family," one wife complained. "But we hardly see him at all. He's with his buddies."

"Did you ask him about it?" we said.

"Yes, but he said it was what he needed right now and I was just going to have to get used to it."

Talk about unnecessary conflicts. Here is a point of contention between two people that could easily be resolved by a simple explanation. The alcoholic might have said, "Honey, they tell me this is what I have to do to stay sober. Don't you want me to do whatever's necessary? Otherwise, what's the point of having gone through treatment?"

Instead, he creates a potential conflict by refusing to discuss it. We asked him why he was being so obstinate. "I am not being obstinate," he said obstinately. "She begged me to go to AA meetings for years, and now that I'm finally doing it, she has no right to say anything. It's none of her business."

Dumb, isn't it? He obviously feels treatment puts him in a one-down position in relation to his wife, and he's expressing his resentment by refusing to talk with her. That's a good example of somebody who thinks he's staying sober for his family's sake rather than his own. This isn't going to work: His anger will build until he finds an excuse to relapse. Back in detox, he'll bitch to the counselor that "I was going to meetings, but she still wasn't happy."

Your friends and family may have made some mistakes in the past, but remember, they didn't know any more about the right way to deal with an alcoholic or addict than you did about how to get and stay sober. No use holding resentments about past errors. Everybody makes them.

So open up the lines of communication with people who have influence in your life. If you're nervous about their response, discuss it with your counselor or self-help group prior to bringing up the issue with someone new. Get their advice and listen to their experiences. And if you get a negative response to frank discussion from someone, discuss this with your group as well. Remember, their opinion is the most important, right now.

Chapter Four

TWELVE STEPS FOR THE NONBELIEVER

THOUGH MANY NONBELIEVERS have rejected Twelve Step groups in favor of alternatives such as Secular Sobriety and Rational Recovery, our experience leads us to believe that most atheists and agnostics recover within the ranks of Alcoholics Anonymous, Narcotics Anonymous, and their sister fellowships. Sound contradictory? It isn't, really. There are a number of practical advantages to attending Twelve Step groups even if you don't believe in a Higher Power:

1. **That's where most of the sobriety is.** From the newcomer's standpoint, the single most important feature of a self-help group is its ability to provide examples of long-term success, in the form of recovering addicts and alcoholics. It's rumored that it required more than two years for the fledgling organization of AA to accumulate one hundred sober members. Once that occurred, however, the success of the organization was almost assured. The initial "one hundred" served as a magnet for other seekers. In the area where we live, many NA members also attend Alcoholics Anonymous, because of the much larger pool of members with more than three years' sobriety—a pool of potential sponsors.

Many of the members of Secular Sobriety, including its founder, achieved their own recovery within the boundaries of a Twelve Step fellowship. The value of this cumulative experience of recovery cannot be overstated.

2. **Twelve Step fellowships are historically very tolerant of different beliefs.** That isn't to say all their *members* are tolerant—they aren't. We've been to meetings where standing up to say you don't believe in God would be regarded as heresy. But we've also seen meetings which appear to be dominated by nonbelievers—meetings where the Lord's Prayer isn't used at the close of the session, and the Steps are interpreted quite differently. For the most part, however, our nonbelieving patients have done extremely well as a minority within Twelve Step meetings largely attended by persons of a more religious bent.

3. **Twelve Step groups usually adapt to include changes in their own membership.** Twelve Step groups have survived where other, better-organized efforts have failed because they adapt to changes in their own membership. Gay and lesbian alcoholics recovered in AA for decades, eventually forming gay and lesbian meetings. New Spanish-speaking meetings arose because of the influx of Latins in New York, California, Texas, and Florida. The appearance of multiple drug users led to the formation of Cocaine Anonymous and toward changes in the traditional membership of both Alcoholics and Narcotics Anonymous. And because the traditions remind the organization of its duty to the alcoholic who still suffers, we suspect that AA and its sister fellowships will continue to adapt to the further changes, as they have throughout their history.

Who knows? In the future we may see "Nonbeliever's Groups" listed in the AA meeting directory.

HOW CAN A NONBELIEVER BENEFIT FROM THE TWELVE STEPS?

Since their inception, the various Anonymous fellowships and the Steps themselves have proved invaluable to people who don't believe in a deity. That's because the Steps have been successfully reinterpreted by thousands of nonbelievers to meet their needs. Sure, there are dogmatists within the Twelve Step movement who insist these individuals are doing things wrong. But the primary purpose of Alcoholics Anonymous is to reach out to the alcoholic who still suffers, and from that perspective, it seems to us that any drinker who can establish and maintain sobriety by using the Steps is using them properly—regardless of how he or she interprets them.

In this chapter, we're going to discuss the Steps from the standpoint of the nonbeliever who is attempting to recover entirely or in part through attending Twelve Step meetings. Instead of giving you a lot of theories about how this should occur, we're simply going to tell you how your predecessors have done it. We know because we've watched them. There's no "right" way, of course. There's only the way (or ways) that work for a given individual.

But first, a bit of background on the Steps themselves. In order to understand the Twelve Steps as they were originally applied to recovery from alcoholism, we should view them in terms of the intellectual and social climate into which they were introduced— the United States in the late 1930s, shortly after the painful, rather spectacular failure of Prohibition.

At this point in history, when the bulk of AA literature was written, the term alcoholism itself was poorly defined. The medical literature contained dozens of complex descriptions of the causes and effects of excess drinking, each in some key way differing from or even contradicting its counterparts. An even greater disparity of meaning was found outside the medical community. For simplicity's sake, we follow the lead of previous authors in dividing this hodgepodge of disparate concepts, theories, and definitions into a few broad categories, called *models,* which reflect the prevailing attitudes toward the problem drinker at the time Alcoholics Anonymous was founded.

THE IMPAIRED MODEL

Many Americans had given up hope that alcoholism could ever be successfully eradicated. They had come to the conclusion that alcoholics were "impaired" by an innate flaw in character which drove them to drink in spite of efforts made to stop them. According to this premise, prevention was a pipe dream and treatment a waste of time and money—a view reinforced by the phenomenal rate of recidivism produced by the primitive treatment methods of the day. Many policymakers developed a caretaker mentality, adopting the position that the only appropriate expenditure of money for alcoholism was in long-term care for Skid Road winos and other terminal cases. If they could not be dissuaded from drinking, society should assume responsibility for minimizing the harm they did to themselves or others.

This model is still quite prominent in America today, and enters nearly every discussion of funding for treatment programs.

THE DRY MORAL MODEL

Religious organizations—especially those with an evangelical bent and a belief in personal redemption—made a positive effort to reach out to the suffering alcoholic, principally relatives of members of their own congregations. Such groups had been the motivating force behind the Abolitionist movement and the now-defunct experiment of Prohibition. They viewed alcoholism as a manifestation of spiritual bankruptcy, moral weakness, and estrangement from God. Accordingly, they emphasized bringing the alcoholic closer to the bosom of the church. In this respect, the Dry Moral approach resembled today's "holistic" philosophies: The sick alcoholic was counseled to alter nearly everything about his life in an effort to leave his past behind him. He might be further advised to marry a good woman, start a family, take a job (often through the church), and testify as to his reformation before the assembled members. Families, in turn, were counseled to nag the alcoholic about church attendance, pour out any alcohol they found in the house, and keep him away from bad associations. The family thus became "policeman" to the alcoholic's drinking—a situation which bred new levels of conflict.

Though the demise of Prohibition seriously damaged this model's credibility, it continued to dominate abstinence-oriented approaches to alcoholism. Its influence can be seen throughout the early writings of Bill Wilson, founder of AA.

THE WET MORAL MODEL

Since the repeal of Prohibition, most Americans (America is, after all, a nation where 70 percent of the population classify themselves as drinkers) have ascribed to the view that people become alcoholic because of a lack of willpower and self-control. Thus, where the Dry Moral model advocated abstinence, the Wet Moral model extolled the superiority of controlled drinking. This emphasis on exerting control over drinking behavior resulted in numerous research attempts to differentiate alcoholic from nonalcoholic on the basis of number of drinks consumed, and in the development of treatment strategies to teach the drinker "when" to stop (a modern example is the media campaign about the importance of "Know When to Say When").

THE OLD MEDICAL MODEL

Over the course of centuries of treating sick and dying alcoholics, physicians and other medical practitioners had developed their own theories about the causes of alcoholism. Many reserved the label "alcoholic" for the most debilitated cases, describing the earlier stages simply as "heavy drinking," at least until the appearance of substantial liver damage. Medical care seldom extended beyond three or four days of detoxification, and patients were customarily discharged as soon as their tremors had decreased to manageable levels. The most severe cases of alcohol-related brain damage were assigned to the back wards of state mental institutions. A favorite tactic was to attempt to frighten the alcoholic into sobriety with tales of disease and death. But most alcoholics failed to respond, and by the late Thirties, many respectable physicians and hospitals refused to accept the alcoholic as a patient.

THE PSYCHOANALYTIC MODEL

The new field of psychoanalysis initially welcomed the challenge of dealing with the alcoholic. Early theories held that alcoholism was the result of inadequate nursing in early childhood, and classified the alcoholic alongside the sexual deviant and the compulsive criminal. The psychoanalyst's enthusiasm for treating alcoholism faded quickly, however, in the face of resistant patients and unpaid bills. Despite its lack of success, the influence of the analytical model can be seen in the modern emphasis on the "addictive personality" and the popular view that alcoholics drink because of psychological conflicts and suppressed feelings from childhood.

The founders of Alcoholics Anonymous—in particular Bill Wilson and Bob Smith—essentially "reinvented" alcoholism, formulating a new concept from their own experience and from bits and pieces of existing theories and beliefs. We call it the *Alcoholics Anonymous Model*. Since both Wilson and Smith had established sobriety using the spiritual and moral precepts of the Oxford Movement, a Christian self-help fellowship popular in England and America in the late nineteenth and early twentieth centuries, it was only natural that spirituality was an integral part of their program from the beginning. The Steps themselves were adapted from Ten Principles by which the Oxfordians tried to live. From the Dry Moral model, Wilson and Smith adopted the belief that alcoholics could recover only by practicing complete abstinence from alcohol. They rejected, however, the Prohibitionist stance and the idea that alcohol itself was inherently evil—it was alcoholism, rather than alcohol, that killed alcoholics.

From the Old Medical model, Wilson and Smith took the notion that the alcoholic was sick and in need of help instead of weak and requiring discipline or punishment. They rejected the Wet Moral emphasis on willpower in favor of turning to a Higher Power, while at the same time acknowledging that the alcoholic did have a choice—between sobriety and death.

From the Psychoanalytic model, Wilson, Smith, and the other founders borrowed the concept of alcoholic as obsessed with alcohol—someone whose preoccupation with alcohol continued during sobriety, fueled relapse, and reflected a variety of character flaws which required ongoing attention and vigilance. If these flaws could be addressed successfully on an ongoing basis, the desire to drink might dissipate.

The new model portrayed the alcoholic as the victim of a physical allergy in combination with a mental obsession. This belief underlies virtually all of the early AA literature. Remember, there was no equivalent of the modern disease concept—no way to view alcoholism as a chronic, progressive, primary disease—to inform their understanding of alcoholism. Instead, they relied on existing schools of thought and in particular, on their own personal experience. That experience taught them one thing that medical science had not been able to demonstrate: that alcoholism, regarded for centuries as largely untreatable, could in fact be arrested. In the Big Book, they went so far as to virtually guarantee success to those who "thoroughly followed our path."

Thus, it's no surprise that the literature of AA contains many references to God, to spiritual understanding, to character defects, to humility, to the "cunning, baffling, and powerful" nature of alcohol itself. In this respect, it reflects its time. We believe it would have been impossible to write about alcoholism or recovery during that era *without* relying on these concepts and this terminology. Had Wilson and Smith written the AA Big Book in 1980 or 1990, it would certainly have used different terminology and discussed alcoholism from a vastly different perspective. And rest assured, the alcoholism literature of the twenty-first century will sound even more different.

With this in mind, let's proceed to our examination of the Steps from the perspective of the nonbeliever. As we go, remember that the Steps are characterized as merely "suggestions" rather than orders or commands. The founders never take the position that theirs is the only way to stay sober. Rather, they view the program that worked for them as an unusually successful way for most alcoholics to remain sober. Anybody who tries to pass the Steps off as holy dictum is dead wrong.

STEP ONE: "We admitted we were powerless over alcohol—that our lives had become unmanageable."

In this initial Step, the founders of AA are simply suggesting you acknowledge that you have lost control over your use of a drug— and that this is having an adverse effect on your ability to manage your affairs.

For the nonbeliever, this presents no particular problem. It's essentially the same thing we asked you to do in Chapter Three (The Sixth Milestone: Self-Diagnosis, p. 62). Except the Steps don't use the term *alcoholism*, or ask you to acknowledge the presence of a disease. There are several reasons for this. First, the term "alcoholic" has too many different meanings, as we discussed above. It's entirely possible for an alcoholic to acknowledge addiction without feeling compelled to take the next logical step toward abstinence (see Chapter Seven, "Experiments with Control"). They'll say, "Sure I'm an alcoholic. That's why I drink. I *have* to."

It's difficult to admit powerlessness and unmanageability, however, without realizing the need to do something about it. If you see yourself as out of control and running amok through your own life, you'll take steps to change that.

Second, alcoholism was (and to some extent, still is) a stigmatized disorder. For some drinkers, it's easier to acknowledge powerlessness than to label oneself an alcoholic. In fact, the Steps avoid the words *alcoholism* and *alcoholic* entirely.

Why is the First Step so vitally important to recovery? Because it provides the motivation for remaining sober. Why would you engage in a program of recovery for a problem you don't believe you have? By completing the First Step, you lay the groundwork for all the work you will do in the future.

Want to try taking a First Step? Complete the following exercise.

Exercise 1

Take a piece of paper. At the top write the heading SIGNS OF POWERLESSNESS AND UNMANAGEABILITY. Then turn to the Bell Chart on page 207, or if you've used a drug other than alcohol as your primary substance, to the Bell Chart for that drug. Ready? Now, look at the events on the downward arm of the chart. Go through them, making a check mark next to each one you've experienced. These events are the symptoms of powerlessness and unmanageability—how you recognize it.

Now, write the first event by which you placed a check mark on the piece of paper. After it write out brief descriptions of one or two examples of that event. For example: "Increased tolerance—I noticed that I had to drink more than I used to just to get the same effect. At Jenny's party in 1984, I drank all night and still didn't feel drunk. My drunk-driving arrest in 1987 was at a BAL of .28, and I didn't feel drunk at all."

Repeat that procedure for each event you checked. Can you see evidence of progression—are things growing worse?

When done, show this to a counselor or sponsor. Get their feedback. Have you minimized or rationalized some events as the product of other forces when they may really have been the result of drinking?

The First Step is seldom complete—as time passes and you begin to understand more about your problem, you'll add new examples of loss of control or continued use despite adverse consequences. Time enhances your perspective.

STEP TWO: "Came to believe that a Power greater than ourselves could restore us to sanity."

Here, the nonbeliever runs into problems. Doesn't a Power greater than the individual refer to God? The standard answer is usually "no—it refers to anything which you perceive as greater than yourself." We've used that explanation ourselves, but we have to admit that from the nonbeliever's perspective, it's nonsense. Of course it means God—not only that, a *Christian* God. The next Step explicitly names God, for Pete's sake. That's obviously how the authors originally intended it to be used.

Fortunately for the nonbelievers who have recovered in AA over the past fifty years, the authors' intention isn't binding. Just as they borrowed and adapted the concept of a power greater than oneself from their Oxford Movement predecessors—changing the meaning as they went—so, too, can the nonbeliever.

Remember: Interpretation of meaning is always relative, and there is no better illustration than the existence of many disparate religious sects and denominations. A Unitarian Universalist and a Jehovah's Witness both pray to God, but their interpretation of God's will couldn't be farther apart. (A joke making the rounds: What do you get when you cross a Unitarian with a Jehovah's Witness? Somebody at your door with very little to say.)

The fact that the founders of Alcoholics Anonymous believed in a Christian God and wrote their literature accordingly does not in any way limit your interpretation of the Steps or your right to use them in your own recovery, to the extent you find them helpful.

After all, the primary purpose of Alcoholics Anonymous is to reach out to the alcoholic who still suffers.

One way nonbelievers make use of the Second Step is simply by emphasizing the importance of having faith in *something outside yourself*. As one nonbelieving patient of ours put it: "I basically rewrote the Step to read, 'Came to believe that faith in something other than my own battered intellect could restore me to sanity.' Though I wasn't sure what would lead me out of alcoholism, I was pretty certain it wouldn't be my willpower. I had learned that from experience."

Look at the logic of that statement. If you've made attempts to control drinking or drug use—and failed—then what evidence is there that you won't continue to fail in the future? After all, the nature of alcoholism and addiction involves continued use despite adverse consequences. Many people who come to treatment do so in the wake of ten or fifty or a hundred unsuccessful efforts to "control" the symptoms of alcoholism. It's defeat which drives them to seek help in the first place. But this same history of failure has left them with a sense of hopelessness that poisons subsequent efforts at recovery. What's the point of seeking help if you don't believe it has a chance of working? Suppose you stopped for three months a couple years back, then relapsed? What entitles you to believe that this time will be different?

Here, alcoholics traditionally resort to *denial*. Faced with a history of failure, the drinker insists that somehow, in some unknown way, this time will be different. His experience contradicts this, but he ignores it. Yet the odds are overwhelming that a few weeks, days, or hours after that discussion, another alcohol-related crisis will occur. After all, how can the same approach that has failed in the past now be expected to yield a positive outcome?

Faith is an entirely different matter. When you have faith, you are simply choosing to believe that somewhere, somehow, you will find the strength to do what you have not done before. Strength not to deny or defeat addiction, but to go to any lengths to recover from it. Strength to do your part—put forth an effort, enter the community that is your group, embrace the group as the "higher power" whose experience and unified strength will carry you through all phases of recovery—and faith that the result you seek will be forth-coming.

Faith also means believing that sobriety will eventually restore you to sanity. Though alcoholics generally have no special premorbid psychological disorders, the experience of alcoholism is enough to give anybody the symptoms of major mental illness. But perhaps you've always looked at alcohol and drugs as your savior—helping you cope, to make it through the day. What will happen now that they're gone?

Will you ever sleep normally again? Will you lose your temper and run over somebody in your car? Find yourself in a suicidal depression? Discover you can't work, function, support yourself?

These are things people think about when they consider giving up alcohol or drugs. *I may be a mess now,* they reason, *but at least I function. I don't know if I can live without drugs anymore.*

Wherever intellect doesn't suffice and the uncertainty of recovery threatens to overwhelm you, resolve to keep trying—that's where faith comes in handy.

Exercise 2

Okay, so you don't believe in God. Fair enough. But you're going to need faith at some point during your recovery. So let's make a list: what *do* you believe in?

Take another piece of paper and write out a list of things you have faith in. Maybe it's your friends, or your family. Maybe it's the support of your group. Perhaps it's the judgment of your counselor or sponsor. Whatever it is, write it down. Then describe briefly how it will help you in recovery.

When you're finished, discuss this with a knowledgeable person.

STEP THREE: "Made a decision to turn our will and our lives over to the care of God *as we understood Him*."

Let's assume you've admitted powerlessness over alcohol and found something outside yourself to serve as a source of strength and guidance through the initial weeks and months of recovery. Now you're ready for the most challenging task of all: permitting this "higher power" to lead you into sobriety.

Suppose you chose your home group as your source of guidance. An issue arises where your desires conflict with the advice of your group. Which do you follow? Your own strong wishes or the counsel of others? It may surprise you to know that your sobriety often depends on the answer to this question.

Suppose you entered a radio contest and were lucky enough to win an ocean cruise. You gleefully announce this to your group. Their response is less than you expected.

"Ocean cruise?" one says. "I been on a couple of those, and everybody stayed drunk the whole time. I stayed drunk for a week."

"I'm not sure you're ready for a cruise," says another. "You haven't been sober long enough. If there's a lot of drinking, you could go off on a bender."

"Slippery places and slippery people," mutters another. "All by yourself, don't know a soul, no telephones except ship to shore. Sounds like a floating cocktail lounge."

You start to get angry. "Look," you say, "you people have a lot of nerve telling me what I can and cannot do. I've been sober three months. I'm working the program. Going to meetings. I finally get lucky enough to win something—first time in my life—and you're telling me not to take it. It just isn't fair."

"We're not telling you to do anything," somebody says. "Just telling you what we'd do if you were us."

"Well I'm *not* you. And just because you can't handle something, doesn't mean I can't handle it. I'm not going to let my life come to a grinding halt just because I quit drinking. I've worked hard, and I deserve this."

Examine the arguments for going: I *deserve* it, I've been *good*, you can't tell me what to do, it's none of your business, it isn't *fair*. It's the tone of a child rebelling against authority, isn't it? As though the group had become a cruel parent rather than something to help you remain abstinent.

They're giving you advice based on their experience; you're rejecting it because it contradicts your sense of the way things should work.

Who knows? Maybe you're right. Maybe you could take that

cruise, have fun, remain sober, have a completely positive experience. But at three months sober, should you really be taking that chance? Suppose you started drinking again? What could happen as a result?

Of course, as the months pass and your thinking clears, your need to discuss every decision with your group diminishes. But relying on your newly healing brain is always a risky proposition.

"Okay, I understand that it will take months for my memory to restore itself, for my thinking to clear, for my denial to recede," the newcomer argues. "I understand that. But here's my problem: what do I do about my marriage?"

Note the false duality in the alcoholic's thinking. On one hand, he realizes the disease has adversely impacted his brain. On the other, he remains preoccupied with marital conflict—one of many manifestations of his illness. He doesn't understand that the reason he cannot effectively solve his marriage problems is *because* his memory is shot and his thinking fogged by alcoholism. He experiences life as an assault by a remarkable variety of problems, one of which is recovery from alcoholism. In reality, *one* problem—alcoholism—is driving all the others. And it's doing so in the most subtle way imaginable: by changing the way you think, feel, and react to everyday life.

That's why outside guidance is required. The language of Step Three asks you to give over your will to the care of God as you understand Him. The trick for the nonbeliever is to take the qualifier "as we understand Him," and transform it into something you can work with, something that makes sense to you. Take a look at the character of the Twelve Step group: It's a community of recovering addicts whose sole purpose—to maintain the sobriety of its members—is inarguably benevolent and positive. The group as a whole is always stronger than its individual members, and it offers hope and support to those who ask for it and are willing to exert the effort recovery demands.

Exercise 3

Make a list of the current problems in your life. They may be in many different areas: problems at home, problems at work, problems in school, problems with the law, problems with your emotions, problems with your health, problems with money. Describe the gist of each in a few sentences. Then restate each problem in the form of a decision you intend to make. Perhaps you'll take action, or seek more information, or study the problem in more depth, or wait and see what happens before you commit yourself.

Done? Now share your list, and the appropriate decisions, with those you have chosen to guide you through recovery. If your decision disagrees with their guidance, then make a conscious effort to do it their way, at least for now.

See if life doesn't start to improve. As time passes, you'll notice your decisions tend to match those of your guides. That's because you're learning from your experience.

STEP FOUR: "Made a searching and fearless moral inventory of ourselves."

The heart of change is self-knowledge, translated into productive action. The heart of self-knowledge is the process of self-examination. By studying your own actions and motives in a structured, insightful way, you begin to free yourself from destructive impulses, tortured emotions, and a false sense of responsibility for the ravages of addictive disease. The Fourth Step guides you down that path.

Moral issues are those having to do with right and wrong, and a *moral inventory* is a way of looking at your past behavior in moral terms. Those who have faith in God and embrace religion receive their moral code from the Church. But morality itself is not linked to any religious system—you don't need to believe in God to know the difference between right and wrong. Nor do you have to believe in God to examine your own character with the kind of rigorous honesty demanded by the Step.

Suppose during your addiction you became estranged from one of your children, the result of years of conflict and bitter resentment on both sides. You can't think of him or her without remembering these fights and getting angry all over again. Yet part of you feels sad at the loss of a relationship with someone you loved, and you wonder if perhaps it was partly your fault. Whenever you think about it, conflicting feelings surface.

That's a proper subject for a moral inventory. You might structure the inventory by asking yourself the following questions, in order:

1) When did these conflicts begin?
2) What usually precipitated our arguments? Was it one or two recurring problems?
3) When the arguments occurred, was I sometimes under the influence, or recuperating from earlier drinking or drug use?
4) Did I usually start the arguments—or "fire the first shot"?
5) Was my child really angry at me because of my drinking?
6) Did I respond to his/her anger in the way I think is best?
7) Now that I understand alcoholism better, was it influencing my behavior in ways I did not understand at the time?
8) Do I see hope of reconciling in the future?
9) Do I feel any remorse over the situation?
10) Is this something for which I would someday like to make amends?

By the time you finished, you would have a much clearer vision of the antecedents and possible solutions to this particular problem. If it's something for which you'd like to make amends in the future, you might file it away for your Eighth and Ninth Steps.

Pay special attention not only to blaming but to the kind of characterological "bad habits" that so often infect the behavior of the practicing alcoholic or addict: perfectionism, unreasonable expectations, impatience with others, a tendency to hold resentments, shame about things you said or did while under the influence. Just as addiction distorts your personality (usually for the worse), so too does recovery often strengthen your character and help you become a better person than before. You can begin the process of dealing with these outgrowths of the disease (what Milam calls *second and third order symptoms*) in the Fourth Step.

Try the following exercise before you move on to Step Five.

Exercise 4: Inventory

Get a notebook and write out a list of all the people, institutions, or forces you blamed for your drinking or drug use. Give this some thought. Did you blame your parents? Your sisters and brothers? Your friends? Your boyfriends or girlfriends? Your husband or wife? Your boss? Your coworkers? The army? The workplace? Your occupation? Or did you blame *yourself*? This will take a while, but be thorough. And be as honest as your brain will permit. If you can't think of any or your list has only four or five items, you're in heavy denial. Do the exercise again. You've been blaming for a long time, and it's sometimes difficult to admit it.

When you're finished, look at each person, place, or thing in turn, and ask yourself the following questions:

1) What makes me think this (person, place, etc.) contributed to my problem?
2) Looking back, do I feel I was right or wrong in my judgment?
3) Why do I feel I was right or wrong?
4) Did I resent or even punish this individual for something which was really the result of my alcoholism or drug addiction?
5) Is this something for which I might eventually want to make amends?

If you have any questions about how to do this, go over the process with your sponsor.

STEP FIVE: "Admitted to God, to ourselves, and to another human being the exact nature of our wrongs."

Now that you've surveyed yourself and begun to identify some of the damage addiction has done to you and to your life, share that with someone else.

Don't be distracted by the Step's suggestion that you first share with God and yourself. For most people (believers and nonbelievers alike), the key to the Fifth Step is your discussion with another person.

Most AA and NA members use their sponsor for this purpose. Some use a clergyman, counselor, trusted friend, or therapist. The Step makes no distinction. You may select any "human being" you want, or more than one. The key to the Step isn't whom you talk with, but what you say to them.

You've probably heard that confession is good for the soul. We're not sure people have souls, but even if they don't, confession is usually good for them anyway. Done properly, it's a fast, simple, and relatively painless way to alleviate feelings of shame.

Shame plays a crucial role in the experience of addiction, though not for the reasons you may think. Go back to Milam's concept of first, second, and third order symptoms. First-order symptoms are the physiological effects of the disease itself, including tolerance and withdrawal as well as the complex "organic brain syndrome" normally found with alcohol and drug toxicity: cognitive deficits, hyperresponsiveness to stress, augmented emotions, perceptual distortion, impaired decision-making capability.

Second-order symptoms are the addict's psychological responses to the first-order symptoms—principally the unconscious defenses which characterize his or her reaction to the anxiety-provoking reality of deteriorating brain function. The five most common defenses are denial, rationalization, externalizing, minimizing, and intellectualizing, but there are a dozen others.

Third-order symptoms are the result of the addict's (and society's) misunderstanding and misinterpretation of what is happening to him. The most common third-order symptom is persistent shame. Alcoholics feel shame not only because of the things they say and do under the influence, but because they are taught to blame themselves, their families, and a host of other problems for being alcoholic in the first place. This springs directly from the societal opinion that alcoholism is a "self-induced" illness.

A counselor provided us with a recent example. Attending a workshop at a local college on medical aspects of alcoholism, she was surprised to hear the physician-lecturer insist that alcoholism was the result of heavy drinking. "Anybody who drinks a lot for seven or eight years will become an alcoholic," he stated. Note the strong implication that alcoholism is therefore the drinker's fault—the result of years of alcohol abuse.

This is a good illustration of the Old Medical model, described in the early part of this chapter. The physician above is assuming that alcoholism is the result of heavy consumption, instead of the cause. In this model, a drinker is required to spend at least a few years drinking copiously to produce alcoholism. But research suggests that just the opposite is true. The alcoholic consumes increasing amounts of alcohol not prior to alcoholism, but *because of* alcoholism. His tolerance requires more alcohol to achieve the same effect others get from a smaller dose. Once addicted, he needs still greater amounts to suppress withdrawal. And when loss of control appears, he experiences compulsions that lead to binges of unpredictable length.

Throughout, Milam's point holds: The alcoholic is responding to the dictates of his physiology, rather than ignoring them. But the Old Medical view ignores this, preferring to hold the drinker responsible for his disease. The implications are remarkable: the drinker is led to believe that if he had only been more responsible, more intelligent, more alert, more health-conscious, better adjusted, stronger of character, *he would not have been an alcoholic*. Is it any wonder addicts and alcoholics are ashamed of their condition? That they will do most anything to avoid the diagnosis? That they respond to the suggestion with horror, resistance, and defensiveness? That they hide their condition from the world? That they treat any attempt at intervention as an assault on their self-respect and integrity?

It's this destructive shame which the Fifth Step helps to relieve. No matter what the alcoholic or addict may have done during the course of addiction, he or she feels most ashamed about the simple fact of being an alcoholic or addict.

But what happens when this reality, in all its ugliness, is shared with another human being, especially a fellow sufferer? Once in the light, things that seemed unforgivable become, well, not so awful after all. Other people have been through it, and come back to tell the tale. If they did it, then maybe so can you.

Obviously, you can't bare your soul to a God you don't believe exists. But you can at least be honest with yourself, and with others.

Exercise 5

Share the results of Step Four with another human being of your choosing. Then discuss the experience of sharing with two additional people you trust.

STEP SIX: "Were entirely ready to have God remove all these defects of character."

Here's another point where people often get caught up (understandably) in the use of the word "God." Our counsel: If you're a nonbeliever, ignore it. Move on to the more important concept of being *ready*.

One common mistake is to assume that change is simply a matter of intention and execution. It might be diagrammed as follows:

$$INTENT + ACTION = CHANGE$$

Alas, all too often it doesn't. People with good intentions take productive action and wind up falling flat on their faces, having to start all over again. That's because they weren't *ready* for change.

Notice we said "for" change rather than "to" change. That's because the real obstacle to lasting, positive alterations in lifestyle and behavior is the "ripple" effect: what it does to the rest of your life.

It's quite simple. When you change any key behavior—especially one so powerful as to qualify as an addiction—it's like tossing a large rock into a pond. It sets up waves elsewhere in your life. If you're not ready for those waves, they can drive you to relapse.

Suppose you were vastly overweight and went on a weight-reduction program. Now you're slender and attractive. When you were heavy, you didn't have to worry about dealing with sexual advances of others because there weren't any. But that's all changed, hasn't it? Everyone is telling you how terrific you look, how excited you must be now at the prospects of your new life. But you're feeling exactly the opposite. "I wish these people would stop looking at me," you think. "How am I supposed to act? I feel like I'm fourteen again."

Months before, when you were considering weight loss, it seemed as though all your problems would be solved once you were the proper weight. Instead, you discovered a whole new set of problems—ones you were much less well prepared to deal with.

The same thing happens to recovering addicts and alcoholics. Unprepared for the reality of sobriety, they often run back to the familiar hell of addiction. "The devil you know," goes the saying, "is better than the one you don't."

For lasting change, the equation should read:

$$\text{INTENT} + \text{READINESS} + \text{ACTION} = \text{CHANGE}$$

How do you attain this state of readiness? Most become "ready" only after a series of earlier failures—the school of hard knocks. But you don't have to go that route if you're willing to put in a little work. Instead of waiting for life to teach you what doesn't work, strive to anticipate—in a structured, insightful, healthy way—the changes that will accompany recovery.

Exercise 6

Get a portable tape recorder and record the following in your own voice, making sure to speak clearly, slowly, and in soft tones. Then find yourself a comfortable chair in a quiet room, and play the tape back, following its instructions.

The tape plays: We're going to do a simple exercise. First, get comfortable in your chair. Place your feet flat on the floor, and your palms on your thighs. Now, take a few seconds to relax and breathe deeply. Make sure you inhale and exhale slowly. (*When recording, pause thirty seconds, then resume talking as follows.*)

Now, picture a television screen. In your hand is a remote control with an on/off switch and a channel changer. Got it? Now, on the television screen, picture yourself as you are now, as though you were watching yourself on TV. Got it? Okay, now imagine yourself as you were during a particularly bad night of drinking or drug use. When you were physically ill, or really depressed, or in a panic about something. Got it? Now picture yourself after six months of sobriety—the way you imagine you will look. Make yourself look good. Pretty impressive, aren't you?

Now, imagine yourself sober, relating to your family. Picture yourself having a conversation with them. What do they say? Are there any problems in this relationship? Are you seeing any conflicts? If so, simply make a note of them—don't try to do anything to change it. It's just a TV show, and you're just watching.

Now, picture yourself at work or school. Who else is in the picture with you? How are they treating you? Any problems or conflicts? If so, take note of them. Don't feel you have to do anything about it—just watch the show, listen to the dialogue.

Picture yourself in two other locations where you spend a great deal of time. Maybe a friend's house, or on a tennis court. Who else is with you? See any problems or conflicts there? (*Pause one minute in reading before resuming.*)

All right. Now use the remote control to switch off the TV set. Relax for a few seconds, making sure to breathe deeply. When you're ready, let your eyes open.

Now get a piece of paper and make a list of how being sober might change your life, for better or worse.

STEP SEVEN: "Humbly asked Him to remove our shortcomings."

Once again, don't get distracted by the reference to "Him." Concentrate instead on the concept of humility.

The experience of addiction is very egocentric. By that we mean the addict must, to support the addiction, progressively ignore the needs of others, including those he or she loves. There's simply no room for them. The demands on time and attention made by addictive disease are too onerous. By the late stages, there's literally no room for anything else. The addict looks at nearly everything (and everybody) in terms of their relationship to his or her consumption of alcohol or drugs.

This egocentricity is often interpreted by others as complete and total selfishness. Paradoxically, family members are often aware of the alcoholic's self-hatred. Thus, the contradiction in behavior expressed by the old AA description of the active alcoholic: "an egomaniac with an inferiority complex."

Humility is the antidote. Humbleness precludes arrogance, self-centeredness, self-absorption. When you do the Sixth Step, you ask for help simply because you need it. You have recognized the necessity of giving up your longstanding practice of perfectionism, of holding resentments, of setting unreasonable expectations on yourself and others, of turning to alcohol or drugs in every crisis. You have also come to believe you cannot remedy this by yourself. You need something other than your own resources.

That's the spirit of the Seventh Step.

Exercise Seven

Take out your Fourth Step inventory and look at the problems it reveals. Have you been a perfectionist, a holder of resentments, etc? Write out your answer. Then discuss this with someone else whose guidance you have decided to seek in recovery. How can you avoid these behaviors in the future? Suppose someone points them out to you. How will you avoid taking that as criticism?

STEP EIGHT: "Made a list of all persons we had harmed, and became willing to make amends to them all."

Here, the Steps leave off the reference to God and once again guide us through the minefields of the past.

In the Fourth Step, we found ourselves rethinking some of our fondest and most enduring beliefs. Perhaps it was a resentment we had always felt was completely justified, revealed by our moral inventory to be the product of diseased thinking. Or perhaps the stress we believed drove us to drink turned out on further reflection to be a byproduct of our own unreasonable expectations, augmented by an addled nervous system. Or perhaps we discovered the most unpleasant truth of all: that we have, intentionally or not, brought great distress to people we care about. We have harmed them, and there is no way to undo that.

It shouldn't come as a surprise. Nearly every recovering person faces this issue at one point or another. It's an inevitable companion to the distorted thinking which characterizes addiction. And every single recovering alcoholic we've ever met feels bad about it.

The Eighth Step advances the first part of a remedy. Instead of wallowing in useless remorse, the Step suggests, make a comprehensive list of all those you harmed during your active addiction. Then become willing to make amends.

The willingness referred to here is close kin to the readiness of the Sixth Step. We interpret it as a state of emotional and psychological openness to the process of change. You perceive making amends not as a duty or obligation but as an *opportunity* to right some old wrongs. You may feel anxious about confronting the past, but you're happy to have the chance.

You're wondering about the nature of the amends? Depends on the situation. For now, we'll leave that issue for the next Step.

Exercise 8

On a piece of paper make a list of all the persons whom you believed you harmed during your active addiction. Start with the most obvious, then go back and add those who come to mind as you work. Describe the situation in which you harmed them and the precise way in which they suffered. If you start to feel guilty or defensive, don't worry about it—these feelings are natural and will pass by themselves. If you find yourself stuck, take a break and come back later, or tomorrow. It often takes a week or more to do this Step properly.

STEP NINE: "Made direct amends to such people wherever possible, except when to do so would injure them or others."

Throughout the Steps, the founders have left several qualifying statements to guide our interpretation of their meaning. The Third and Eleventh Steps used the phrase "God as we understood Him" to remind us that there is no one way to define "God" and individual variance is not only acceptable but desirable. In the Ninth Step, the authors again qualify their suggestion about amends with the caveat about avoiding injury to other people.

It's an important point. Making amends often means going back into the past and apologizing for things you said or did during painful or even crisis situations. That's difficult enough, but it can actually prove harmful if you don't examine the potential problems inherent in a dramatically altered situation.

Here are examples of the right and wrong way to do Step Nine. These are taken from actual cases, though we've changed the identifying characteristics. Note the difference in approach. We'll start with the wrong way to do the Ninth Step.

Fran, age thirty-seven, felt great remorse over her behavior in an earlier relationship with a man which had ended about a year before she stopped drinking and using drugs. Their torrid affair had come to an end when his wife, having hired a detective to uncover their relationship, confronted them in a restaurant and, as Fran put it, "totally went bonkers," screaming epithets, throwing crockery, and threatening to amputate her husband's genitalia. Afraid of the prospect of divorce and the loss of his children, the man broke off the affair. Fran, feeling betrayed and deserted, went on a three-week drinking binge, at the end of which she showed up at his house in the middle of the night and broke all the windows. When her lover and his wife came running out, Fran tried to run them down with her Volkswagen Beetle and wound up crashing into a telephone pole, which resulted in her second drunk-driving arrest.

At six months sober, Fran decided it was time to make amends for her behavior, and for having tried to break up a family with four young children. Her sponsor was less confident.

"I dunno, Frannie," she said. "You don't know for sure how things are between them. The little woman sounds pretty volatile."

"I need to do it, Sue," Fran replied. "It's preying on my mind, interfering with my sobriety."

Still, Fran didn't want to see her ex-lover's wife unless she absolutely had to. She contemplated calling him first, but decided that would put him in an awkward position if his wife should find out they met. If she came unannounced, his wife couldn't be angry with him for agreeing to meet Fran. The responsibility would be hers.

He was in fact completely surprised by her appearance. "You look fabulous, Frannie," he said, as they hugged. She spent half an hour telling him about her new life in AA, her revived career as an actress, and her newfound commitment to humility and unselfishness. He told her something about the struggles his marriage had been through since they last saw one another, and when he finished, Frannie apologized for her earlier behavior. "Really, I understand," he assured her. "It was a crazy time for everyone, and we were both drinking too much. It was as much my fault as yours."

Feeling like a fifty-pound weight had been lifted from her back, Fran got up to bid him goodbye. They hugged for a last time, and to Fran's surprise, the hug turned into a rather passionate kiss. When they broke, Fran saw that he, like she, knew they would never see the other again. She felt a tear run down her cheek as she turned to go.

But at the door of the office stood her lover's wife, a look of pure horror on her face. Before Fran could say anything, the woman ran screaming from the building, her husband in pursuit. Fran stood by herself, thinking, *what have I done?*

Fran's error lay in not anticipating the possible ramifications of re-entering what was once an explosive situation. She overruled her sponsor and plunged ahead in her usual self-centered, impulsive fashion. As a result, her efforts to heal had resulted in new wounds on top of the old.

Now the right way. This situation is if anything even more complex than Fran's, but note the difference in the way the recovering addict approaches the problem of contacting his old friend, and the criteria by which he judges his actions.

Bennie, age forty-two, had been sober more than a year when he decided to make amends to his former employer, from whom he had embezzled more than $100,000 during his four years of employment—most of it to pay for cocaine. Bennie felt horribly remorseful about his behavior because this man, an elderly immigrant, had treated Bennie like a son, bringing him into the business with little experience and entrusting him with responsibility for the payroll. Worse still, when the embezzlement had finally been discovered and the firm's accountants had pointed the finger at Bennie, by then in a halfway house for addicts, the old man had refused to press charges and insisted to any and all listeners that his friend Bennie would never have robbed him under any circumstances.

Bennie told his sponsor about this incident during his Fifth Step and expressed his concern at the prospect of making amends. "It's even worse than it sounds," Bennie explained. "Because the old man defended me and the cops couldn't prove I did it, I was never prosecuted. Which means I got away with stealing more than a hundred thousand bucks. If it gets out, I could go to jail for a long time. I could live with that, but I know how cops think, and they'll probably assume he was in on it. Even if he isn't prosecuted, the papers will drag his name through the mud."

"Jeez, Bennie," the sponsor said, "this is like a soap opera."

"I know. He's a wonderful old man, but he is 88 years old and he has a temper. Maybe I shouldn't say anything, just let sleeping dogs lie."

"If you could do that, Bennie, I doubt we'd be having this conversation in the first place."

Bennie agonized for months before finally coming to a decision. "Here's what I'm going to do," he told his sponsor. "I'm going to go see the old man at a time and place where I know we'll be alone. I'll tell him I want to make amends, and that some of the stuff I have to say might really upset him and could even get us both in big trouble. So if he doesn't want to hear them, I'll keep it to myself and never tell a soul till the day I die."

The old man was overjoyed to see Bennie, told him how well he looked and how it made his heart glad to see him off drugs for good. Their conversation proceeded as Bennie expected, and when the moment came, he told his former employer that there were some things he wanted to reveal, adding the warning just as he had rehearsed it.

The old man looked at him with amusement. "You want to tell me a secret, Bennie?" he said. "What is it, that you stole all the money?"

Bennie was astounded. "You knew?"

"Of course. You think I got Alzhammer's disease or whatever they call it?"

"But why did you defend me?" Bennie stammered. "I mean, I took a hundred grand . . ." He winced as he said the words.

"One hundred forty one thousand, eight hundred sixty dollars," the old man snapped. "And some odd cents."

"You knew all along . . . why didn't you turn me in?"

The old man beamed. "Because you are a good boy, Bennie, and that counts a lot more than money. Besides, you were in the drug program, and if I let the police have you, you would rot in some prison, which would do nobody any good. I know, I've been in prisons myself, in the old country."

"How do I ever repay you?" Bennie said. "I feel like I'm more in your debt than ever."

"You don't have to repay me. Just do something for somebody else, when you find them in trouble. Give them a chance, like I gave you."

Simply by thinking about the welfare of others rather than himself, Bennie maintained the spirit and intent of the Ninth Step—and benefited as a result.

Exercise 9

Take the list you made for the Eighth Step and beside each name, write whether or not you feel a desire to make amends to this person, and secondarily, whether you think it is possible at this point in time. Remember, making amends isn't a time limited proposition; many people make amends over the course of years, as the opportunities present themselves. There's no big rush.

Now: wherever you indicated that it was both possible and desirable to make amends at this time, make a plan for doing just that. Look at each situation in terms of the potential harm you might inadvertently bring to others. Discuss this with your sponsor. When you agree on the best approach, proceed with your amends.

STEP TEN: "Continued to take personal inventory, and when we were wrong, promptly admitted it."

Steps Ten, Eleven, and Twelve are sometimes called the "maintenance" steps. You've done the initial work of identifying the flaws which feed relapse and letting go of remorse over your addictive past. Now you must concentrate on maintaining the gains you have made.

Step Ten advises that you continue the process of taking inventory. It doesn't tell you how or how often to do this, but most try to take inventory on a daily or weekly basis, asking themselves: "am I living according to the principles of the Steps?"

The Step also suggests prompt admission of wrongdoing—a concept unfamiliar to most of us, alcoholics and nonalcoholics alike. We're proud of our willingness to stand up for what we believe is right, but in reality we also frequently defend ourselves even when we know we haven't got a leg to stand on. We even go so far as to develop complex webs of defense mechanisms and sometimes even alternate personalities to hide from ourselves the fact that we are involved in something wrong. And yet it is the nature of human existence that more often than not, we find ourselves in error.

Maybe we misjudged a situation, relied on false or insufficient information, proceeded on false assumptions, committed ourselves to a position we later regretted taking. In the past, we'd have tried to tough it through, hoping no one discovered our error, relying on our overdeveloped defensive skills to divert attention from the mistakes we made. That's part and parcel of addiction. But that's all behind us now, and this Step advises us to avoid taking that position.

Instead, it suggests that we evaluate ourselves by the simplest of standards: were we right or wrong? And if we find ourselves on the bad side of that question, just admit it. No fuss.

It's deceptively powerful. If you don't fight your own conscience, you soon feel better about yourself, and avoid conflicts with others, too.

Exercise 10

Schedule a daily session by yourself, in which you evaluate the events of the week in terms of right and wrong. If you discover you were wrong about something, admit that to the appropriate person. Then forget about it.

STEP ELEVEN: "Sought through prayer and meditation to improve our conscious contact with God *as we understood Him*, **praying only for knowledge of His will for us and the power to carry that out."**

Okay, as a nonbeliever, you're not going to be doing a lot of praying, and there's no reason you should, because as many AA members will testify, it isn't necessary. You can meditate instead.

Meditation is one of those practices which almost everyone describes as helpful yet to which relatively few of us devote the requisite time and attention. There are numerous studies which seem to indicate a positive benefit from simple daily meditation for anyone dealing with a difficult life problem—from executives under stress to entertainers preparing to perform to prisoners in confinement to persons recovering from alcohol and drug addiction. Nobody is absolutely certain how it works, but for most people, work it does.

Think of meditation as a way of bringing yourself into contact with your feelings, restoring your sense of inner balance and revitalizing yourself for contact with the outside world. Meditate to rid yourself of your daily accumulation of tension and disturbances, allowing you to keep in close contact with the things that really matter.

If you're skeptical about all this, it's probably because you never had the chance to think about what meditation really is. It's not magic. It's just an extremely effective way to establish a reasoned and rational sense of self that is unaffected by crisis and conflict—building strength that will carry you through whatever comes your way.

The only way to find out if it works for you is to try it. Here's an exercise.

Exercise 11

Do the following exercise every day for ninety days. Try not to miss a single day, but if you do, don't make a big deal out of it. Just go back to daily meditation.

Find a quiet place, where you can be free of distraction for about twenty minutes. Because meditation tends to energize you a bit, most people meditate in the early morning or late afternoon, after work or school. Get in a comfortable position. It could be on a mat or cushion on the floor, or in a comfortable chair. Place your hands palm up on your thighs.

Now, begin deep breathing. It's best to emphasize the exhale rather than the inhale, so try the following: inhale to a count of three, bringing the air all the way down into your stomach, so you can feel your diaphragm pressing against your belly. Hold for a count of one, then exhale for a count of nine, flushing the air from your body by contracting your stomach until you feel "empty." Then take another breath and repeat the process. Try it ten or fifteen times. Make sure you get all the air out before you inhale. You might feel a warm or tingling sensation—that's good. It means you're relaxing.

After a few minutes of breathing, when you feel you have the knack and are into the rhythm of abdominal breathing, begin to recite, either softly to yourself or silently, the following sound: *shur-ring*. If you want, you can start by reciting it out loud, then switch to hearing it in your thoughts. Say it over and over, at whatever interval feels right. There's nothing magical about the sound, so if there's one you like better, go right ahead and use it.

Many things—pictures, scenes, feelings—will flow through you, but it isn't necessary to respond to them. Just keep repeating the sound. If you prefer to have something to watch with your mind's eye, you can also picture the flame of a candle flickering in the dark. See if you can, by thinking about it, steady the flame.

After about twenty minutes, or when you feel done, open your eyes, stretch, and return to what you were doing.

STEP TWELVE: "Having had a spiritual awakening as the result of these Steps, we tried to carry this message to alcoholics, and to practice these principles in all our affairs."

Of all the Steps, this one, along with the First, is probably the most crucial to ongoing sobriety. A lot of people in Twelve Step fellowships stay sober simply by practicing Steps One and Twelve.

Many people have said that the key to AA's success with addicts is the recognition that if one addict is trying to help another stay away from drugs and alcohol, at least the one who's doing the helping probably won't relapse. If nothing else, it would be too embarrassing.

Maybe that's why AA groups often give responsibility for making coffee or renting a meeting space or finding speakers to members with relatively little sobriety. As one says: "I think they figured that if I was sitting in the middle of the bench, it would be a lot harder to fall off."

Perhaps it's why the fledgling organization of Alcoholics Anonymous went into the back wards of hospitals to carry the message of recovery to alcoholics on whom everyone else had long since given up. Maybe they were hoping for a miracle, or maybe they were doing it for their own benefit.

Probably it's why when a newcomer realizes exactly how much time and effort an older member has poured into him, asking nothing in return, and tries to thank the older member, is told: don't thank me. I'm doing it for my own sobriety. If you want to repay me, give of yourself to someone with less sobriety than you.

Twelve Step groups operate on the principle that the best way to keep your own success is to give it away to someone else. By being generous with themselves, AA members restore their own faith in the power of recovery, and build another wall between themselves and the next drink, joint, or hit. In sharing the strength you've received from the community, you actually deepen your faith in the group spirit that has fostered your recovery. Once again, like the Steps themselves, this principle is both deceptively simple, and deceptively powerful.

Exercise 12

Each day, look for the opportunity to share your recovery with someone else—especially those who need it most. Think of it as a privilege rather than an obligation. In fact, strive to view life itself in exactly the same way.

Chapter Five

TWELVE TRADITIONS FOR THE NONBELIEVER

TO UNDERSTAND HOW NONBELIEVERS are able to make use of (and thrive within) a spiritual program such as that of Alcoholics Anonymous, we must study the peculiar way in which such groups are organized. Don't make the mistake of thinking that Twelve Step fellowships are just therapy groups without a professional leader. They're not. They operate on a different plane altogether, according to principles not always fully understood by their own members. These guiding principles are set forth in yet another collection of suggestions from the founders of Alcoholics Anonymous—the "Twelve Traditions."

Note the use of the word *tradition* instead of rule or commandment. In the language of group dynamics, a tradition is a way of doing things that arises not from the demands of an outside authority but from the experience of the group itself. By adopting a certain practice as a tradition, the group saves itself from the dilemma of forcing each of its offspring to solve the same problems over and over again.

The Traditions of Alcoholics Anonymous reflect the early (and often painful) learning experience of its founders. Not coincidentally, these Traditions provide for diversity among the membership and safe haven for those who desire help with alcoholism—including nonbelievers.

THE FIRST TRADITION: "Our common welfare should come first; personal recovery depends on AA unity."

Many scholars regard Alcoholics Anonymous as one of the great social movements of the twentieth century. They may be right. But from our perspective, the great achievement of AA isn't to be found in the lessons of the Twelve Steps, or the Big Book, or in the message of recovery and hope which AA members present to the public at large. The real miracle of AA is its survival.

There have been literally thousands of organizations launched with a good cause, the best of intentions, and considerable resources, only to fail. Alcoholics Anonymous itself borrowed much of its structure and philosophy (including the Twelve Steps) from the Oxford Movement, a Christian self-help group which subsequently collapsed. Groups which sprung up like wildfire in the 1980s, such as the Adult Children of Alcoholics movement, may be all but forgotten in another decade. Such movements fail for many reasons. Sometimes the cause that gives birth to them fades in importance. Sometimes they are assimilated into other, more enduring movements. But by and large, the most common reason for the failure of such groups is the selfishness of their own members.

We're not saying there's anything necessarily destructive about self-interest. But there is a contradiction inherent in social movements that are formed to benefit their own members. Suppose the interests of some members contradict the larger interests of the group? Which should prevail? Should the needs of the individual be sacrificed in favor of the whole? If so, isn't that contrary to the reason most members joined the group in the first place?

This question was hotly debated in the early years of AA, and the Tradition represents the solution arrived at by the original membership. Where something threatens AA as a whole, unity of the group must take priority. Why? Not because of some abstract principle of altruism and self-sacrifice. Simply because it is their experience that without the group, the members cannot remain sober. They've tried innumerable times. And since failure usually results in eventual death, the group *cannot* be sacrificed for the interests of a member. Ultimately, that would contribute to the destruction of everyone else.

THE SECOND TRADITION: "For our group purpose there is but one ultimate authority—a loving God as He may express Himself in our group conscience. Our leaders are but trusted servants; they do not govern."

From the nonbeliever's standpoint, this is the most controversial of the Traditions, because it refers to God as the ultimate authority. But once again, the founders add a qualifier: The expression of God must come through the "group conscience," a sort of moral election wherein the membership of a given AA group decides the "right" action to take based on the principles of the organization. If you believe in God, then this conscience reflects the will of the deity. If you don't, then it expresses the will of the group, struggling to draw a moral conclusion. Most nonbelievers find this an acceptable alternative.

One mystery is why AA uses the term "Higher Power" rather than "Highest Power," which would have been the expected phrase. Then again, in view of the vast numbers of people claiming to speak for God, perhaps this isn't so strange after all.

The key point of this Tradition, of course, has to do with the prohibition against government. Nothing contradicts our modern concept of the successful organization more than the existence of one with more than one and half million members, no real authority, no bureaucracy, and no set of policies and procedures. Alcoholics Anonymous went so far as to adopt the most inefficient form of government yet devised: the group consensus. This reliance on group agreement to decide nearly every question of consequence virtually guarantees that no one within AA will ever amass any sort of political power, or gather the strength to alter AA's primary purpose—which is to reach out to the alcoholic who still suffers.

THE THIRD TRADITION: The only requirement for membership is a desire to stop drinking.

AA went through a period of experimentation before arriving at this Tradition. Earlier versions of the Big Book tried to limit mem-

bership to those with an "honest" desire, but in a disease characterized by denial, who can say he or she is being honest about
anything related to alcohol?

Still, this Tradition turns out to be crucial for those who, because
of their beliefs or background, represent "minorities" within AA—
including atheists and agnostics. The Tradition welcomes you, and
with the word "only," specifically bars its own members from setting
additional conditions on membership.

THE FOURTH TRADITION: Each group should be autonomous except in matters affecting other groups or AA as a whole.

Here, the founders decentralize the organization by giving each
group (there are tens of thousands) the right to self-determination
in all but a few larger issues. That also accounts for the remarkable
degree of variation found among meetings. In many Baltimore-area
groups, for example, the meeting begins with the reading of the
Preamble; in northern Virginia, just seventy miles away, meetings
usually start with a prayer. Groups can and do decide on their own
size, the language the meeting is conducted in, the place where they
meet, the format of the meetings, and who they are trying to attract.
This individual sovereignty works well for the nonbeliever—it gives
you a vast selection of groups to choose from.

The group is your key to sustained sobriety. With an investment as
important as this, it's incumbent upon you to shop around until you
find the group that fits most comfortably. Reasonable investigation
on your part is perfectly acceptable. After all, if you're confident
that you've placed yourself in the right environment, your participation is likely to enhance the strength of the group.

THE FIFTH TRADITION: "Each group has but one primary purpose—to carry its message to the alcoholic who still suffers."

Here is the organization's statement of its commitment to the principle embodied in the Twelfth Step. AA members are taught that
sobriety is best attained not through self-help but through helping

others—as the phrase goes, "the best way to keep it is to give it away." Some newcomers are stunned when other members or their sponsors advise them during their own darkest hours to find someone with still worse difficulties, and offer your services to them. And yet, it seems to help. Try it yourself. Next time you're in the middle of a crisis, and things look worst . . .

THE SIXTH TRADITION: "An AA group ought never endorse, finance, or lend the AA name to any related facility or outside enterprise, lest problems of money, property, and prestige divert us from our primary purpose."

From the beginning, it was clear that money, business, and finance were not compatible with the spirit of the Twelfth Step. An aborted attempt to gain financing for a string of AA-owned treatment centers led the founders to the conclusion that AA worked best on a level of corporate poverty.

THE SEVENTH TRADITION: Every AA group ought to be fully self-supporting, declining outside contributions.

How then would AA pay its own expenses—maintain its telephone switchboards, publish its literature, keep its central office open? The solution was passing the hat. "You can donate a million dollars to AA if you so desire," went the saying, "but it has to fit in the hat."

That's why no matter how much Alcoholics Anonymous has done for you, or for your family, you'll never receive a letter which begins, "Dear Friend of AA, it's time for the annual Fund Drive . . ."

THE EIGHTH TRADITION: "Alcoholics Anonymous should remain forever nonprofessional, but our service centers may employ special workers."

Just as Tradition Six kept AA out of the treatment business, Tradition Eight prohibits AA from certifying counselors or giving its blessing to any particular treatment method. Though many professionals in the addiction field are members of AA, they leave their professional role at the door and become fellow sufferers. The "special workers" AA employs are simply to man the phones, fill orders for books, and take care of other basic needs where volunteers can't.

THE NINTH TRADITION: "AA as such ought never to be organized but we may create service boards or committees directly responsible to those they serve."

Once again, the basic unit of Alcoholics Anonymous, remains the meetings themselves; no bureaucratic superstructure may develop.

THE TENTH TRADITION: "Alcoholics Anonymous has no opinion on outside issues; hence the AA name ought never to be brought into public controversy."

This is a very difficult policy to maintain, because when members see alcoholics being mistreated by the public health or corrections system, they want AA to step in and lead the fight for justice. But the founders believed that controversy detracted from the organization's credibility, making it less effective in reaching the alcoholic who still suffered. Thus, though members can and do take positions on many outside issues, they are enjoined against doing so as a representative of AA.

THE ELEVENTH TRADITION: "Our public relations policy is based on attraction rather than promotion; we need always maintain personal anonymity at the level of press, radio, and films."

Here's a Tradition frequently broken, especially since the influx of entertainment and sports celebrities into treatment centers. Once again, the Tradition exists because the founders believed that undue publicity—even good publicity—could scare away newcomers who might otherwise have accepted the help of AA. And the primary purpose of AA is . . . well, you know.

THE TWELFTH TRADITION: "Anonymity is the spiritual foundation of all our traditions ever reminding us to place principles before personalities."

Here you see the real intention of anonymity. Contrary to popular belief, it isn't to preserve confidentiality, or to protect members from persecution or stigma should their involvement be discovered. It's to protect the members from the promise of reward or benefit—those twin demons which sabotage humility and lead people away from the group's real purpose. In a way, it's like the saints who insisted on being buried in unmarked graves, so they couldn't be deified or even venerated. We can argue the merits of such thinking, but it's hard to fault the principles it represents.

In closing, the very lack of structure inherent in Twelve Step fellowships is a prime source of their appeal to the nonbeliever. The group's goal is simply to help one another remain sober.

Ultimately, the Twelve Step movement isn't about God, but about finding the strength to overcome a fatal disease. And that's something best done in the company of fellow travelers.

Chapter Six

ADDICTION MADE SIMPLE

MOST NONBELIEVERS ARE SKEPTICS in the truest sense of the word: willing to challenge any assertion or assumption not clearly founded in observation and fact. Given their nature, it's no surprise they feel frustrated by the literature on alcohol and drug addiction. As one complained, "Most of the books I've read don't even bother to define alcoholism. And the literature on families is even worse. I read one author who gave twenty-three definitions of codependency! And he seemed to think this was a good thing!"

His wife chimed in, "I do think my husband is overcritical, but I have to agree he has a point. Maybe some people can take these things on faith, but to ask someone to change his whole life based on something that the so-called experts can't even describe in an understandable fashion—well, that's expecting too much."

We agree. That's why we'd like to take this opportunity to explain exactly what we mean by alcoholism and drug addiction, and how it works. By the way, if you find yourself with questions or disagreements as you read, jot them down on a piece of paper and discuss them with counselors or other knowledgeable persons. If all else fails, send them off to us care of the publisher, and we'll answer to the best of our ability.

Why would we take the time to do this? Because if you don't understand addiction, your recovery will be tainted by false hopes and unreasonable expectations—no matter how intelligent or sincere you may otherwise be. So take your time, pay attention, and by all means, ask questions.

Our goal is not just to give you a lot of new information you can parrot back on a quiz. It's to provide you with the basis for making the all-important *paradigm shift*, away from your old way of thinking and toward a new understanding of your experience in terms of a chronic, progressive, and potentially fatal disease.

Accordingly, let's begin with the most basic question of all.

IS ADDICTION A DISEASE?

Yes. Surprisingly, this has been the subject of much controversy, all the way up to the Supreme Court. Yet if one understands the term *disease*, it quickly becomes apparent that argument is unnecessary.

To determine if something is a disease, we need only ask if it fits the accepted definition of that term. It's a simple process which becomes difficult because the medical profession and the lay community use the word in different ways.

Most people think of a disease as something with a clearly identifiable physical cause, such as a virus, and an obvious medical treatment, such as surgery. By these standards, addiction doesn't appear to qualify. After all, what do victims of some terrible disease like cancer have in common with people who drink too much? Most of us go through adult life using alcohol occasionally, in moderation—why should we feel sorry for people who overindulge? And the same argument is used against the drug addict: If an individual chooses to experiment with dangerous, illegal substances, then whatever happens as a result is their own fault, right? Doesn't calling them "sick" wrongly absolve them of responsibility for their problems, and for the harm they do to others?

Besides, the argument continues, the primary treatment for alcoholism and drug dependence is abstinence—an act of will. What other disease can be cured with willpower? The cancer victim cannot will a halt to the runaway growth of cancer cells. The heart patient cannot command his blood pressure to drop. Opponents of the disease model contend that if alcoholism were caused by a virus or a genetic defect and its treatment included pills and injections, then they would agree it should be reclassified as a disease. But because it doesn't, they can't. Case closed.

Yet this string of arguments against the disease model is based entirely upon our willingness to accept a narrow, restricted definition of disease. That's a fatal flaw. In medicine, "disease" is regarded as an *inclusive* rather than an exclusive term. There are a wide variety of legitimate medical disorders—some of our biggest killers, in fact—which would have difficulty qualifying as diseases under the definition used above. Thus, it's no coincidence that much of the criticism of the disease concept comes from outside the field of medicine, from the world of law and social philosophy, where "disease" is a seldom-used, foreign concept.

Most medical texts define disease in terms of three features:

a) it's **morbid,** meaning bad for the victim,
b) it's a **process** rather than a single episode, and
c) it has characteristic **signs and symptoms** which may be used for purposes of identification.

By these standards, a great many conditions qualify as diseases. That has a utilitarian value in medicine, because newly identified or poorly understood disorders must be classified as diseases long before much is known about their causes or outcome. Why? So that physicians and other medical professionals can treat them.

Think of it this way: If you view addiction as a crime, you send the addict to jail. If you see alcoholism as a crisis in faith, you take the alcoholic to church. If you look at addiction as a disease, however, you bring its victims to a doctor. And because addicts and alcoholics suffer all sorts of medical problems that can't be treated through legal or spiritual interventions, this is absolutely essential.

So for the purpose of this discussion, let's view the issue the way a physician might. Ask yourself: Do alcoholism and drug dependence fit the criteria for inclusion as a disease?

1) **Is addiction morbid?** This is easy—there are few disorders more likely to result in premature death. Not only does addiction kill directly, through overdose, accident, and liver failure, but also as

a hidden contributor to dozens of other serious diseases. Ask a coronary care nurse what percentage of her patients die of alcohol-related heart attacks. Talk to those who work with AIDS patients about the contribution of untreated alcoholism or addiction to the spread of HIV. If we include nicotine among the addictive drugs (which the Surgeon General insists we do), we're into some really enormous numbers—more than a thousand Americans die each day from tobacco-related illnesses.

2) **Is addiction a process?** Another emphatic yes. Many people become addicts in their teens or early twenties and remain that way until their deaths—for some, more than fifty years later. In fact, each stage of addiction seems to build upon the last. Alcoholic fatty liver matures into cirrhosis. Occasional bouts of intoxication as a young man become the frequent binges of middle age. The cumulative effect of years of assault with alcohol and drugs is enormous, and can be measured using a variety of medical tests and psychological scales.

3) **Does addiction have characteristic signs and symptoms?** No arguments here—go to your local library or bookstore and you'll see shelves of books on recognizing the signs and symptoms of addiction. A sign, by the way, is something that can be objectively measured, while a symptom is usually a subjective complaint by the patient. Every medical and nursing student learns to recognize addiction before graduation, and struggles to cope with its effects for the rest of his or her professional career.

There's usually a caveat in medical dictionaries: Something may be a disease regardless of whether the etiology (the cause) or the prognosis (the probable outcome) is known. In fact, clinicians normally recognize and describe a disease a long time before researchers positively identify its cause. AIDS is a recent example. Before HIV was discovered, many people believed AIDS was transmitted through a common stimulant known as a "popper," which had become popular among gay men. And even if we hadn't discovered the cause of hypertension or melanoma or diabetes, they would still be diseases, and require treatment.

Thus alcoholism may qualify as a disease regardless of whether or not the cause has been absolutely determined. Indeed, if we look closely at the broad categories of coronary heart disease and diabetes, we see they actually have a great deal in common with addiction, as illustrated by the following chart.

	Alcoholism	Heart Disease	Diabetes
1. Chronic	X	X	X
2. Potentially fatal	X	X	X
3. Many patients require intensive medical care	X	X	X
4. Treatment involves behavior modification	X	X	X
5. Disease can be arrested rather than cured	X	X	X
6. May be more than one sub-type	X	X	X
7. Varies in extent and severity	X	X	X
8. Environmental factors contribute	X	X	X
9. Predisposition is hereditary	X	X	X
10. Mechanism of inheritance not yet determined	X	X	X

Note especially the significance of number 10: in fact, it is *rare* for medical science to understand the precise method by which a chronic disease is transmitted within a family. Yet the experimental and statistical evidence for heredity is so persuasive that prevention efforts may be successfully targeted on the basis of genetic risk.

Obviously, alcoholism fits neatly into the company of chronic diseases. A number of common psychiatric conditions also qualify: schizophrenia, depression, or bipolar disorder, for example. In fact, many alcoholics and drug addicts also suffer from concurrent medical and psychiatric disorders.

Try thinking of a broad category of "addictive disease" which includes addiction to a variety of substances. Though all forms are chronic and primary, there will be dramatic differences in personal experience depending on an individual's preference for a given drug. If your body becomes dependent on alcohol rather than PCP, for example, you're much more likely to wind up hospitalized with liver disease, because alcohol is remarkably toxic. On the other hand, if your drug of preference is cocaine, there's a better chance you will go bankrupt than if you became an alcoholic, simply because the compulsive use of cocaine is very expensive. The process of addiction, however, retains its basic characteristics, and you can't give up one drug in favor of another.

That's the mistake made by many cocaine addicts who renounce cocaine but secretly intend to continue having the occasional drink. It never occurs to them that one night they'll get drunk and forget why they stopped snorting coke, or wind up getting in trouble with alcohol.

WHY DO PEOPLE DRINK AND USE DRUGS?

One persistent point of confusion concerns the question of why alcoholics drink and addicts use drugs. The underlying assumption, made from what noted author James Milam calls the *psychogenic paradigm*, is that people who become addicted have all sorts of hidden psychological problems which motivate drinking and drug use. If this secret anguish can be uncovered and dealt with in therapy, then the motivation for drinking will disappear. Yet as Milam argued in his book *Under the Influence,* alcoholics start drinking for about the same reasons as everyone else.

You can demonstrate this yourself with a simple exercise. Take a pencil and write below all the reasons that people give for drinking alcohol. Not just the ones that you use, but those you've heard from other people. Keep your list simple (example: "to relax"; "to socialize"), but try to come up with at least ten.

1.
2.
3.
4.

5.
6.
7.
8.
9.
10.
11.
12.
13.

Finished? Now, go through your list and put a check mark next to those which you believe are the reasons that only an *alcoholic* would give. For instance, if one of the reasons you have listed is "to get drunk," and you feel that only alcoholics set out specifically to get drunk, then put a check mark by that entry.

If you're like most people, your completed list probably looks something like this:

1. To relax
2. To feel good
3. To relieve stress   √
4. To socialize
5. To increase confidence
6. Like the taste
7. Routine (certain time or situation)
8. For medicinal purposes
9. To fit in with your peers   √
10. To celebrate
11. Part of romance
12. To get drunk   √
13. To stop the shakes   √

But if you examine those reasons more closely, you can see that each and every one could be (and often is) used by alcoholics and nonalcoholics alike, with the exception of number 13, which is peculiar to the alcoholic. Alcoholics routinely drink for all the above reasons. They, like their nonalcoholic brethren, enjoy the taste, the feeling, the social uses of alcohol. And nonalcoholics also drink to relieve stress ("Hey, can we stop somewhere for a drink? I've been on the go since eight this morning.") and do sometimes deliberately set out to get drunk (remember college? The military?).

If you like, substitute cocaine, heroin, or another drug for alcohol. Your list should be about the same. Once again, the only real difference between addict and non-addict is reason number 13. Sure, you might want to replace the shakes with cocaine craving, but the motivation is just as strong. And withdrawal isn't obvious until addiction is well in place.

Alcoholics and non-alcoholics share many common motives for consuming alcohol. The only one they don't share—the need to suppress withdrawal—normally becomes a factor only later in the addiction process. It's a sign that alcohol and drug use has become medicinal rather than recreational—and that the alcoholic or addict now has difficulty functioning without the substance.

ARE ALL DRUGS EQUALLY ADDICTIVE?

No, but let's explain what we mean by that. Despite the fact that most addicts and alcoholics have used a variety of substances, they develop definite preferences which persist throughout the course of addiction. Preference is determined biologically, by the strength of your body's response to a given drug. There are four basic categories of preference:

Aversive: Some drugs, though classified as addictive, may make you sick or uncomfortable. It's unlikely you will use them beyond initial experimentation.

Mild Positive Response: Other drugs might evoke some pleasure but not enough to keep you coming back. You might use these only in certain settings.

Moderate Positive Response: These are drugs you use regularly because you like their effects, but which you do not regard as your "drug of choice."

Strong Positive Response: The substances (usually only one or two) to which you are most attracted.

If you've used a number of different substances in your life, try the following exercise. Use the space below to make a list of *all* the mood-altering drugs you've ever consumed, divided into the afore-mentioned four categories.

Mild Positive	Moderate Positive	Strong Positive	Aversive
1.	1.	1.	1.
2.	2.	2.	2.
3.	3.	3.	3.

When finished, look at the drug or drugs you've entered in the "strong positive" column. Are they stimulants such as cocaine or amphetamines, or depressants like alcohol, narcotics, or tranquilizers? One theoretical model holds that the brain's pleasure centers of each individual's brain are genetically programmed to prefer stimulants or depressants. This may explain why some addicts drink heavily during cocaine binges but experience little or no alcohol craving at other times, or why many alcoholics have experimented with cocaine but have little desire for further use.

When we calculate the "addiction potential" of a substance, we're looking at the percentage of experimenters who go on to develop the symptoms of addiction. About 10 percent of drinkers become alcoholic, while we estimate that about fifty percent who try crack eventually become addicts. We therefore conclude that crack is "more addictive" than alcohol. In fact, crack seems to have greater addiction potential than snorted cocaine. What's the most addictive drug of all? Probably the common cigarette. Studies indicate that about half of the people who try it experimentally go on to become heavy smokers. That may seem confusing unless you think of nicotine as an addictive drug and the cigarette, pipe, or chaw as different methods of ingesting it, similar to snorting, shooting, or smoking cocaine.

IS ADDICTION HEREDITARY?

Yes. But that may not mean precisely what you think. Since this is another subject of controversy, let's take the opportunity to explain the relationship between heredity and environment in some detail.

Some diseases (Huntington's disease is a tragic example) work through simple inheritance. If you are unlucky enough to inherit the Huntington's genes from your parents, you will inevitably contract the disease. But more complex diseases normally require some contribution from the environment as well as the genetic predisposition. The risk of coronary heart disease, our number-one cause of death, is greatly increased by behaviors such as smoking or overeating. These behavioral factors serve to *provoke* the expression of heart disease.

In the case of alcoholism, the "environmental provocation" comes from regular drinking. It's quite possible to inherit a predisposition to alcoholism but drink so infrequently that you never develop the disease. This is not uncommon in families where one or both parents are alcoholic; the experience of being raised by a drunken father or mother often turns their children into teetotalers. But suppose your familial history was a generation or two removed—a grandparent or great-grandparent, perhaps. You may be largely unaware of your risk.

Addiction and heart disease aren't alone in requiring contribution from the environment. Though some forms of diabetes are strictly genetic in origin, there are a number of environmental risk factors such as obesity, alcoholism, and lack of exercise that contribute to the development of the disease.

The evidence for heredity in addiction is persuasive. Let's review some of the principal studies.

ANIMAL STUDIES

By mating rats with a preference for alcohol, T. K. Li of the Indiana School of Medicine was able to produce offspring who were genetically programmed to drink to intoxication and who experienced withdrawal when alcohol was removed. Other strains have been bred to abhor alcohol. That's a strong indication that the key to alcohol preference in animals is genetic rather than environmental.

TWIN STUDIES

Studies of identical and fraternal twins are useful in determining heredity because scientists can measure the concordance (occurrence in both members) of a trait, even when raised apart. Research in Sweden and Finland showed that if one identical twin was alcoholic, the chances that the other twin would have the disease were very high even if the twins were adopted in infancy and raised in separate families. Of course, the environment plays a role here as well. Suppose one twin grew up in a family that practiced abstinence, while the other was raised by heavy drinkers. That, too, would affect the eventual risk for alcoholism.

ADOPTION STUDIES

The best way to differentiate between nature and nurture is through the time-consuming method of studying children born to parents with a particular trait, then adopted in infancy and raised in an adoptive family where that trait was absent. For example, Donald Goodwin and his associates selected a number of Danish subjects with alcoholic biological fathers and nonalcoholic adoptive parents, and compared them to another group where the natural parent was nonalcoholic and the adoptive family included a drinking alcoholic. He discovered that the risk for alcoholism in the adopted sons of alcoholics was several times greater than in sons without the alcoholic family history—regardless of the environment in which they were raised. Goodwin's research was followed up by a number of other adoption studies, most getting their data from the superb health record systems found in the Scandinavian nations.

One such study was conducted by Robert Cloninger of Washington University in St. Louis. Cloninger's vast research found that not one but two types of alcoholism seemed to run in families (See Figure 6-1). The more common Type 1 seemed to represent the majority of alcoholics found in America's treatment programs—higher functioning, less disposed to criminal behavior, more stable in employment, a significant percentage female. Type 2 alcoholics, on the other hand, dominated the criminal justice system, and were overwhelmingly male. A third category (Type 3), was identified by Marc Schuckit to include alcoholics who also suffered from Antisocial Personality Disorder. As you might imagine, this Type also

FIGURE 6-1

Cloninger's Types of Familial Alcoholism

Type One (Late onset)	Type Two (Early onset)
Affects both males and females	Mostly males
Early onset	Later onset
Milder symptoms	Severe symptoms
Slow progression	Rapid progression
Few arrests	Multiple arrests
Influenced by environment	Not influenced by environment

experiences frequent difficulties with the law. It's possible that alcoholics found in correctional facilities may have quite different family histories than those in private treatment centers.

A large American adoption study undertaken by Remi Cadoret of the University of Iowa has found similar sub-types among a population of drug abusers. Surprisingly, the "milder" Type 1 form seems to correlate with a family history of alcoholism while the more severe Type 2 is perhaps linked to a familial background of other drug addiction. All the studies have found an increased risk for addiction in adopted children, as much as five generations removed from a familial alcoholic.

BIOLOGICAL MARKERS

A number of studies have found measurable differences in response to alcohol, not only in the alcoholic but in the offspring of alcoholics. Henri Begleiter of the State University of New York compared a group of boys seven to thirteen years old, all of whom had alcoholic fathers, with a group of boys of the same age without the alcoholic parent. They found striking differences in the amplitude of the P3 wave, an electrophysiological indicator. Alcoholics also show impairment on the categories test, which measures the ability to recognize patterns in a visual field.

This was assumed to be the product of alcoholic drinking until experiments found similar deficits in nondrinking sons of alcoholics. Still another experiment using electroencephalographic readings found that sons of alcoholics experience increased alpha activity after drinking, leading them to feel subjectively more relaxed than their peers, and perhaps providing a "rebound" sensation of irritability once the alcohol wears off.

Another promising avenue of research involved cAMP, a substance which can be identified through ordinary blood tests and which may prove a reliable indicator of alcoholism, even of the less severe Type 1 (who so often goes undiagnosed because of a high level of functioning).

Kenneth Blum of the University of Texas Health Sciences Center regards alcoholism as a disorder of the "reward cascade," the brain's pleasure mechanism. Alcoholics produce greater quantities of TIQ (a brain substance which closely resembles morphine) and therefore, he believes, have a greater propensity for addiction. In Blum's model, the alcoholic's experience of alcohol is significantly more pleasurable than the nonalcoholic's—and the absence of alcohol is perceived as quite uncomfortable.

Thus heredity and environment should be viewed as partners in the creation of addictive disease. The contribution of each may vary from individual to individual, but both invariably play a role. We use the term *environment* to describe the various cultural and familial inducements for drinking or drug use. We have not seen any persuasive evidence to convince us that there exists an "addictive personality" which leads to addiction—indeed, we have seen quite a bit of research which indicates that the personality characteristics usually associated with alcoholism are a product of the disease rather than the cause.

In order to tease apart the relationship between alcoholism and the psychiatric symptoms which so often accompany it, researchers had to undertake prospective or longitudinal studies of remarkable magnitude and duration. The most famous of these was conducted under the auspices of Harvard University and summarized by George Vaillant in his 1983 book, *The Natural History of Alcoholism.* The study began in 1940, spanned some forty years in the lives of its subjects, and focused on two groups: Harvard sophomores (most from middle- and upper-class backgrounds) and boys of the same age from the largely immigrant, blue-collar areas of south Boston. Subjects underwent batteries of psychological tests and psychologists used the results to predict later problems, including alcoholism.

The study found no significant premorbid differences in personality between those who later developed alcoholism and those who remained social drinkers. The traditional psychoanalytic explanations of alcoholism (oral personality, et al.) were discredited. Moreover, the character defects ordinarily associated with alcoholics—insecurity, low frustration tolerance, bouts of depression, among others—were clearly the result of years of alcoholic drinking rather than its cause. Though alcoholics usually showed evidence of a variety of psychological problems while drinking and during detoxification, in most cases those abnormalities were reduced by half at the end of an initial year of abstinence. At three years sober, it was once again difficult or impossible to distinguish the recovering alcoholic from the non-alcoholic through psychological testing.

Before we move on, let's try a simple tracing of your family history. Using the chart below, or one of your own making, list the members of your family in the appropriate generation. You may have to do a little research into your family tree first. We've provided an example of a typical family profile, using the fictional family of Alice Alcoholic as an example.

Current Generation (List yourself and all siblings, and note any whom you believe may have a drinking problem.)

1. Alice
   Female   33   Problem drinker; 1 DWI arrest
2. Naomi
   Female   30   Nondrinker; stable
3. Frobish
   Male   26   Drug addict and alcoholic, treated twice for addiction.
4. Tullah
   Female   24   Social drinker; treated for depression
5. Nigel
   Male   21   Social drinker, occ. marijuana

Parents' Generation (List your parents and their respective siblings.)

Mother's Side
1. Alice's mother (Gwendolyn)
   Occasional drinking bouts; never treated

2. Sister Georgina
   Abstainer; religious reasons
3. Brother Glyphus
   Unknown; no family contact since late teens

Father's Side:
1. Father (Burton)
   Heavy drinker but no loss of control
2. Brother Berthold
   Unknown; no contact with family
3. Brother Blinster
   Unknown drinking habits

Grandparents' Generation

Mother's Side
1. Grandfather
   Moderate drinker
2. His brother Mark
   Unknown
3. Brother Matthew
   Unknown
4. Sister Fatima
   Unknown
5. Grandmother
   Nondrinker
6. Her brother Luke
   Severe alcoholic
7. Her brother John
   Heavy drinker

If you have adult children of your own, you might also want to profile their drinking practices. One caveat: Alcohol and drug problems were heavily stigmatized until the middle of the twentieth century, and families went out of their way to keep it a secret from the outside world, and even from their own children. There may be a number of "skeletons" in your family closets, unbeknownst even to your parents or grandparents.

Borrowing Cloninger's model, Alice's family look like Type 1: both males and females are vulnerable to addiction, with alcoholism running on both sides of the family. Younger brother Frobish's case looks more severe than his older sister's, and one sister is an abstainer—common in families adversely affected by alcoholism. Tullah's depressive problems may represent an independent disorder (which may also run in this family) or simply a response to a difficult situation. Nigel, the "baby," shows no sign of loss of control—yet. Remember, too, that even though alcoholism runs in families, the majority of children of alcoholics do not become alcoholic themselves. You'll find families with an alcoholic parent but no alcoholism among the offspring, and families where nearly every member develops the disease. But statistically, about one in four eventually becomes alcoholic.

Note also the number of "lost contacts": that's also characteristic of alcoholic families. The reason children lose contact is usually because of their own drinking or their desire to distance themselves from someone else's problems.

If Alice's family had been Type 2 or 3, we'd have seen a preponderance of male alcoholics, probably in trouble with the law at an early age. But as a female, her own risk would have been decreased.

There are also differences between various ethnic populations. The percentage of alcoholics among Native Americans and Eskimos, for example, is far greater than that found elsewhere in America, while among those of Asian and Jewish descent the disease is relatively rare. There are a number of biological and cultural explanations to choose from, but the observation applies only to alcohol: Some of the worst drug epidemics in world history have occurred in Asia (opium in China in the nineteenth Century, amphetamines in Japan after World War II).

DEFINING ADDICTION

Now we're ready to look at the issue of definition. Though alcoholism clearly qualifies as a disease, its definition has been modified several times. That in itself isn't unusual. Diseases are frequently redefined as new knowledge becomes available, or as new classification systems are put into effect. This is especially true in psychiatry, where our understanding of the brain chemistry which underlies behavior leaves much to be desired, and diagnosticians must rely on observations of behavior rather than laboratory tests to identify disorders. As our understanding becomes more complete, whole categories of psychiatric illness have been eliminated from diagnostic manuals. *Neurosis* is a perfect example. Though hundreds of thousands of individuals were treated for various neuroses in the past, the last two decades have seen the concept of neurosis virtually disappear from use, replaced by other, more descriptive terms.

At one point, there were over one hundred separate definitions of alcoholism in the literature, ranging from the all-inclusive ("drinking so as to cause problems") to the overly restrictive ("drinking more than three drinks per day for a period of longer than three months") to the entirely speculative ("drinking to self-medicate underlying emotional conflicts"). All had serious flaws. If you use the inclusive definition, then everyone ever arrested for an alcohol-related offense would qualify, despite vast differences in behavior. To borrow an old example, suppose you're drinking a martini and choke to death on the olive. Should the coroner write "alcoholism" on your death certificate?

Many researchers have fallen into the trap of "drink counting," setting imaginary lines based solely on consumption. But some drinkers suffer physical and psychological harm on a relatively small amount of alcohol. Others drink only sporadically, with extended periods of abstinence between binges. Still others limit the number of drinks while failing to include the times they "freshen up" a drink. And the last mistake—made by psychiatrists all over the world—was to separate addict from nonaddict by motivation, as we illustrated in our little exercise on why people use alcohol.

Probably the first real breakthrough in a workable medical definition of alcoholism came in 1976, as a result of work by the National Council on Alcoholism in cooperation with American Medical Society on Alcoholism. That "NCA Definition" was clear, concise, and objective enough for clinical use. We quote the introductory paragraph: "Alcoholism is a chronic, progressive, and potentially fatal disease characterized by tolerance and withdrawal, and/or pathological organ change." *Chronic* means long-lasting. *Progressive* means worsening over time, especially when one symptom contributes to the development of another, as enlarged fatty liver does to eventual cirrhosis. *Potentially fatal* implies that having alcoholism shortens your predicted life span. We can illustrate that by comparison.

The average life span of a male in America today is about 74 years. If we confine ourselves to men with cardiac problems such as hypertension, the life span probably drops into the early sixties. If we look at men with diabetes, it's probably the late fifties. If we select only men with alcoholism, it's about fifty-two years.

That doesn't mean every alcoholic dies before age fifty-five—if it did, some of you would not be reading this. It does imply that for every alcoholic who lives to eighty, there's another who doesn't make it to age forty. It's important to understand that only a minority of people with alcohol and drug problems ever receive treatment for addiction. Most simply die of its complications. If you've been treated, you're in a privileged group.

The NCA definition was revised in 1990 by the renamed National Council on Alcoholism and Drug Dependence and the American Society of Addiction Medicine. The revised version is "Alcoholism is a primary, chronic disease with genetic, psychosocial, and environmental factors influencing its development and manifestations. The disease is often progressive and fatal. It is characterized by continuous or periodic impaired control over drinking, preoccupation with the drug alcohol, use of alcohol despite adverse consequences, and distortions in thinking, most notably denial." Note the statement about the etiology of alcoholism, which reflects the tremendous increase in research knowledge (particularly about genetics), which has occurred over the past fifteen years. Note also the shift from emphasis on physical dependence toward the more subjective areas of loss of control and cognitive distortions.

A psychiatrist making a diagnosis of alcohol or drug dependence, however, will make use of a set of criteria developed specifically for that purpose. Psychiatrists, for example, diagnose with criteria found in the *Revised Diagnostic and Statistical Manual of Psychiatric Disorders* (commonly abbreviated DSM-IIIR). In the case of alcoholism, for instance, those criteria include the following:

1. Alcohol taken in larger amounts and over longer periods than intended. This is usually a sign of *compulsion* (see page 154 for discussion), an increased desire for the drug after initiating use. Many people mistakenly define compulsion as needing the drug to function (that's dependence), thinking about the drug all the time (that's obsession), and using the drug without forethought (that's *im*pulsive).

2. Persistent desire or efforts to cut down or control consumption. Normally a reflection of increasing withdrawal leading to loss of control (see page 154). Alcoholics develop what Milam calls "control strategies" to restrict their drinking to appropriate settings. After a while, however, the disease undermines these resolutions. Eventually, most alcoholics go on the wagon for brief or extended periods, usually to prove to others that they are not alcoholic. It doesn't occur to them that an alcoholic who isn't drinking is still an alcoholic, as demonstrated by the experience of millions in Alcoholics Anonymous.

3. An inordinate amount of time spent in activities necessary to obtain, use, or recover from the substance. The alcoholic's preoccupation with alcohol (he may run out of milk, but not out of beer) gradually develops into an obsession which dominates his life. By the later stages, he spends most of his waking hours drinking, thinking about drinking, or fighting a hangover. When he sleeps, he dreams about liquor.

4. Frequent intoxication or withdrawal symptoms which interfere with the ability to fulfill major obligations, or drinking when it is physically hazardous. More signs of loss of control and increasing withdrawal. He can't go to the party because it's in the evening and he's too drunk; he can't go to work because he's shaking and vomiting. Maybe he carries a six-pack in the car and drinks as he drives.

5. Important social, occupational, or recreational activities given up or reduced because of drinking. As the disease progresses, the alcoholic's life becomes increasingly restricted by the demands of withdrawal. Socializing without alcohol becomes increasingly difficult, and socializing while drinking leaves one vulnerable to lapses in control and perhaps obvious drunkenness. Eventually, the alcoholic stops going out altogether, or confines her associations to carefully controlled situations where she is less likely to get into difficulties.

6. Marked tolerance: a need for increased amounts in order to achieve intoxication or the desired effect, or markedly diminished effect with continued use of the same amount. This is discussed in detail on pages 143–146. The alcoholic's tolerance permits him to "function" (albeit in an impaired fashion) despite the consumption of what might otherwise be toxic doses.

7. Characteristic withdrawal symptoms. Withdrawal normally begins before the level of alcohol or drugs in the bloodstream reaches .00. Thus, many alcoholics experience craving for a drink or discomfort due to withdrawal while still technically under the influence of alcohol. See pages 146–148 for discussion.

8. Alcohol often taken to relieve or avoid withdrawal symptoms. The advent of "medicinal" rather than "recreational" drinking. By this point the alcoholic is no longer drinking to "get high," or experience euphoria. He or she is simply seeking a blood alcohol level high enough to allay the symptoms of withdrawal and permit him or her to function.

Before we discuss these and other symptoms in detail, let's take a simple test designed to help us "self-diagnose" possible alcoholism or drug dependence. Answer the following questions as truthfully as possible. Remember, nobody is looking over your shoulder—this is between you and a fatal disease. Be as honest as you can.

SELF DIAGNOSIS INVENTORY

1. Do you feel your drinking is at all abnormal?   YES   NO
2. Does anyone ever complain about your drinking?   YES   NO

3. Do you ever argue with anyone about your drinking?
   YES   NO
4. Have you ever made an effort to conceal your drinking from others?   YES   NO
5. Do you believe that your drinking causes problems for other people?   YES   NO
6. Do you ever have difficulty recalling all or part of something that happened while you were drinking?   YES   NO
7. Have you ever felt guilty about your drinking?   YES   NO
8. Have you ever felt you were being unfairly criticized because of your drinking?   YES   NO
9. Do the people around you regard your drinking as normal?   YES   NO
10. Have you ever been arrested for an alcohol-related offense?
    YES   NO
11. Have you ever driven under the influence, to the point where you worried about being picked up by police?   YES   NO
12. Have you ever become severely intoxicated?   YES   NO
13. Do you frequently continue to the point of obvious intoxication?   YES   NO
14. Have drinking or drugs ever contributed to the loss of a friendship?   YES   NO
15. Have drinking or drugs ever contributed to the loss of a love relationship?   YES   NO
16. Have you ever been to a meeting of AA, NA, or CA?
    YES   NO
17. Have you ever been assessed by a professional for a problem in which alcohol played a role?   YES   NO
18. Have you ever promised to cut down, only to return to your previous level of consumption?   YES   NO
19. Have you ever promised to quit, only to break your promise?   YES   NO
20. Have you ever had problems at work in which drinking or drugs played a role?   YES   NO
21. Have you ever been treated psychiatrically for a problem to which drinking or drugs may have contributed?
    YES   NO

22. Have you ever continued to drink or use drugs despite the knowledge that it would probably lead to undesirable consequences?　YES　　NO

23. Have you ever experienced difficulty stopping once you began?　YES　　NO

24. Have you ever consumed considerably more than you originally intended to drink?　YES　　NO

25. Have you ever been told that alcohol or drugs have in some way damaged your health?　YES　　NO

26. Has a doctor ever diagnosed alcohol or drug-related problems on a physical examination?　YES　　NO

27. Have you ever experienced nausea or vomiting following a drinking or drugging episode?　YES　　NO

28. Have you ever experienced shaking or extreme nervousness the morning after a drinking or drugging episode? YES　　NO

29. Have you ever experienced insomnia or sleeplessness which was remedied by drinking or drugs?　YES　　NO

30. Have you ever sought advice or help for a drinking or drug problem?　YES　　NO

31. Have you ever neglected family, social, or work obligations because of drinking or drug use?　YES　　NO

32. Can you always stop without a struggle?　YES　　NO

33. Has anyone in your family ever sought advice about your drinking or drug use?　YES　　NO

34. Has anyone in your family ever complained about your drinking or drug use?　YES　　NO

35. Are you always able to stop drinking when you want to? YES　　NO

36. Have you ever sought advice from a clergyman about a problem in which alcohol or drugs played a part? YES　　NO

37. Have you ever been involved in a fight or argument when you were drinking?　YES　　NO

38. Do people around you ever comment on the amount of alcohol or drugs you consume without appearing drunk? YES　　NO

39. Do you feel that you are able to consume more than most people without obvious intoxication?   YES   NO
40. Have you ever made an unsuccessful attempt to quit? YES   NO

Total the number of "yes" responses. If there are more than three, you are probably alcoholic or drug dependent, pending diagnosis by a physician who specializes in addiction. He or she will attempt to ascertain not only the presence of the disease, but its severity.

Now we're ready to take a closer look at some of the signs and symptoms we've been discussing.

TOLERANCE AND PHYSICAL DEPENDENCE

In practical terms, tolerance means the ability to consume large or increasing amounts of a substance without the obvious symptoms of intoxication, such as stumbling, staggering, or slurred speech. An elevated tolerance permits the alcoholic or addict to function under the influence of toxic doses. Tolerance is normally the product of metabolic, neurological, and behavioral adaptation to the effects of a drug.

Metabolic tolerance is the result of the body's efforts to process alcohol and drugs more efficiently. Alcohol metabolism occurs in the following steps:

Ethanol
Acetaldehyde
Acetic Acid
Water and Carbon Dioxide

Simply put, the initial step (ethanol into acetaldehyde) occurs because of the presence of enzymes including alcohol dehydrogenase (ADH), and the second step because of aldehyde dehydrogenase (ALDH). The average person has sufficient quantities of these enzymes to metabolize about three-fourths of an ounce of

alcohol consumed over the course of one hour. That's approximately the amount found in a single standard serving of beer,
wine, or liquor. If we drink more than this amount, we will experience a degree of "intoxication" (literally, alcohol poisoning). These
effects are not unpleasant, because the brain is simultaneously getting a euphoriant (pleasure-producing) message. Nevertheless, the
body is already struggling to cope with the toxins produced by
alcohol.

There is a "back-up" system of enzymes, however, which the liver
sometimes utilizes to handle larger amounts of alcohol and which
helps to explain the alcoholic's phenomenal ability to consume the
drug. The Microsomal Ethanol Oxidizing System (MEOS) is not
based on a finite quantity of ADH or ALDH. Instead, it accelerates
the rate of metabolism in response to increasing quantities of alcohol consumed. In other words, the more you drink, the faster your
liver breaks it down, and the sooner its effects wear off. That's why
alcoholics sometimes consume doses large enough to keep them
unconscious for two days only to find themselves awake four hours
later, craving another drink.

Neurological (or central nervous system) *tolerance*, on the other
hand, reflects the brain's efforts to make efficient use of the quick
energy provided by alcohol without suffering cell damage from its
toxic effects. Alcohol is an efficient source of caloric energy, easily
accessed because it doesn't have to pass through the digestive tract.
Like the rest of the body, the nerve cell first becomes alcohol-
preferring, then alcohol dependent, requiring greater and greater
doses to achieve the same effect. The final factor, *behavioral tolerance*
describes the process by which the alcoholic learns to compensate
(or cover up) his or her intoxication.

Put these three together, and you have a person who can "function" under the influence of remarkable doses of alcohol or a drug.
For example, most medical texts contain a chart describing the
relationship between blood alcohol level and predicted behavior in
the drinker. Let's compare the response at a given blood alcohol
level for a nonalcoholic drinker and for an alcoholic with the dramatically elevated tolerance characteristic of the middle stages of
this disease.

NonAlcoholic	BAL	Alcoholic
No effect	.00	Withdrawal discomfort
Decrease in motor skills	.05	Some relief from discomfort
Legal intoxication	.10	Calm enough to drive
Obviously drunk	.15	Appears relaxed, "sober"
Severely intoxicated	.20	Mild intoxication
Stupor	.25	Obvious intoxication
Coma	.30	Severe intoxication
Minimum lethal dose	.35	Stupor
Death (50% of cases)	.40	
Death (100% of cases)	.60	

Remarkable, isn't it? In our clinical practice, we have seen several cases of alcoholics with blood alcohol levels above .60 who were admitted to detox—*awake*. The highest recorded blood level in a patient who survived is 1.5, roughly twice the level believed to be universally fatal.

With this in mind, alcoholic behavior becomes much more understandable. The outsider's traditional confusion over the alcoholic's motives ("Why drink so much? Why not stop at two drinks like other people?") is revealed as simple ignorance. Alcoholics consume as much as they do because their alcoholic physiology requires that amount to obtain the desired effect. Alcoholics drink as frequently as they do because their bodies punish them if they don't. Their response to alcohol is as abnormal as the diabetic's to sugar.

But never forget that the nature of alcoholism sometimes permits the alcoholic to perform amazing feats of skill and motor coordination while under the influence. For example, a few minutes after a close defeat in a recent twelve round world championship bout, a professional boxer was found to have a blood alcohol level of .06— meaning he was undoubtedly legally drunk for most of the fight.

It's ironic that corporate presidents and school administrators cite high performance as evidence that their employees are drug- and alcohol-free. The nature of addiction is to permit—even encourage—the addict to function at a fairly high level despite the ingestion of toxic doses of a chemical, until the disease reaches the stage where it begins to create the kind of problems that motivate change. That's why addicts and alcoholics seldom seek help until the addiction is well advanced. When a patient brags about catching his addiction early, we almost always respond, "No, you didn't." That's because early-stage alcoholics and addicts aren't found in treatment programs. They're out in the world at large, drinking and using drugs, setting the stage for their own eventual collapse.

ANATOMY OF WITHDRAWAL

Withdrawal syndromes vary from drug to drug, but like mood-altering drugs themselves, can be divided into two broad categories: *depressant withdrawal* (alcohol, sedatives, narcotics) and *stimulant withdrawal* (cocaine, amphetamines, caffeine, and nicotine). Acute withdrawal from a depressant normally lasts three to six days, features marked physical discomfort, and should be supervised by a physician. The symptoms of stimulant withdrawal, on the other hand, are never as severe as those of heroin or alcohol but wax and wane over a period of several weeks, promoting relapse through persistent craving.

The initial symptoms of depressant withdrawal include the following:

Anxiety
Insomnia
Irritability
Nausea
Headache
Diarrhea
Sweating
Muscle Aches
Cramping

For obvious reasons, these symptoms are normally most pronounced in the morning and fade as the day progresses. Most addicts and alcoholics fail to recognize them as signs of addiction and instead misdiagnose themselves as suffering from a cold, a viral infection, or even a simple hangover. Indeed, it is difficult to differentiate withdrawal from a variety of ordinary illnesses until it progresses to the more severe mid-level symptoms, as in the following examples.

Anxiety becomes *panic*. A panic attack is characterized by rapid pulse, sweaty palms, and the sensation of "butterflies" in the stomach, often for no identifiable reason. Many addicts, troubled by such symptoms, are misdiagnosed by their physicians as suffering from panic disorder and medicated with sedative hypnotics, which they take in combination with alcohol despite the risk of overdose. Still others incorrectly diagnose themselves as "phobic" and retreat from the world, never realizing that their "friend and solace" (alcohol) is the real culprit.

Insomnia turns into *fractured sleep* (multiple awakenings) or true sleeplessness which once again is often incorrectly medicated by the unsuspecting physician with cross-addictive hypnotics such as Halcion, Dalmane, or a barbiturate.

Irritability becomes first the "inner shakes" that addicts describe as "feeling like you're going to vibrate apart any minute now" and eventually the visible *tremor* for centuries associated with alcoholism. A number of unrelated conditions can cause tremor, but alcohol and drug withdrawal is particularly noted for its ability to produce an "intentional" tremor, which is most exaggerated during a purposive activity such as writing or picking up a cup. In the popular film *The Verdict*, Paul Newman, playing an alcoholic attorney, trembled so badly he could not pick up a shot glass of whiskey without spilling most of it. In the great tradition of alcoholic problem-solving, he simply bent over the glass and lapped the liquor like a dog. As his blood alcohol level rose, of course, his hands steadied and he was able to hold the glass.

Skid Row "winos" reputedly invented the "towel trick," which permits the tremulous drinker to consume alcohol from a bottle he cannot hold. Wrapping a towel or scarf around the bottle and looping the other end behind the neck, the drinker employs a crude pulley to bring the lip of the flask to his mouth without spilling it.

Nausea eventually becomes the trademark *vomiting* associated with the morning after an episode of drinking or drugging—what noted speaker Father Joseph Martin calls "the lifelong association with the toilet bowl." Of course, by that point the alcoholic has probably ceased regular eating and experiences "dry heaves."

Headache turns into the *migraine*-like pain normally treated by the alcoholic or addict with still more medications, usually prescription narcotics. For female addicts, migraine is normally associated with pre- or post-menstrual discomfort.

Sweating becomes the fabled *night sweats*, where the addict awakes during the night to find himself drenched in his own perspiration, as if he had just taken a shower. If alcohol is involved, this sweating is often mistaken for evidence of recent drinking. A manager once complained bitterly about his secretary "reeking of alcohol at work," when in reality he was smelling her perspiration during withdrawal—a sign that she *hadn't* consumed alcohol recently.

Muscle aches and cramping are particularly common in narcotics withdrawal, and may be compared to an unusually severe case of the flu.

A small percentage of depressant addicts experience *hallucinations and convulsions*. The most common hallucinations are bugs and snakes, and are usually associated with alcoholic hallucinosis or delirium tremens. Convulsions occur when the nervous system is so overburdened with undischarged electrical energy that its only hope of reducing stress is through a seizure. Such convulsions are by themselves harmless unless the alcoholic suffers from a cardiac condition, and often result in a clearing of the sensorium.

Once tolerance and dependence are established, the alcoholic or heroin addict frequently falls into the *maintenance* pattern, where drinking or drug use is daily (and almost continual) and the goal of consumption is not to get high but to stave off painful withdrawal. Once in this pattern, addicts and alcoholics often consume enormous quantities of alcohol or drugs for years or even decades, while continuing to "function" at work. Though legal intoxication is .10 in most states, you probably know someone (though perhaps you're not aware of it) whose blood alcohol level never gets *down* to .10. (See chart on page 145.)

FIGURE 6-2

The Maintenance Pattern

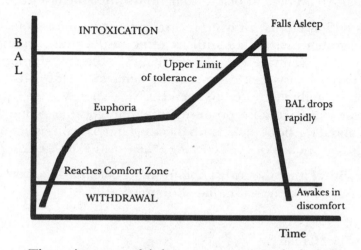

The maintenance drinker consumes enough alcohol to maintain a blood level above the point where withdrawal begins, but strives to avoid visible intoxication. Note the high tolerance that hides the signs of drunkenness from others, except perhaps late at night.

Stimulant withdrawal follows a very different course. There are a number of models of cocaine withdrawal in the literature, but the one which most closely matches our clinical experience is the following:

Stage Zero: *Toxicity*

Begins: While using, addict reaches level of cocaine poisoning.

Signs & Symptoms: paranoia, irritability, restlessness, anxiety, hypervigilance, repetitive-compulsive behavior, and perhaps cocaine-related seizures.

Ends with: User runs out of cocaine, usually has conscious desire to stop.

Stage One: Panic

Begins: An average of one to four hours after the last dose.

Signs & Symptoms: Craving for drug returns; resolutions to stop are forgotten. Associated with extreme restlessness, agitation, inability to concentrate on other activities, obsessive thinking, and what psychologists call "drug-seeking behavior" (DSB)—the addict will be strongly motivated to spend or steal money, barter or trade possessions, make false promises to obtain cocaine. Some addicts crawl about the floor picking up pieces of lint or crumbs in mistaken belief they are bits of rock cocaine ("hoovering" or "geeking").

Ends with: Either the addict obtains more cocaine or is overcome by the onset of withdrawal-induced depression.

Stage Two: Crash

Begins: Twelve to twenty-four hours after last dose.

Signs & Symptoms: Principally depression, often accompanied by suicidal thoughts or feelings. One television anchor recalls sitting in his car with his shotgun barrel in his mouth and his thumb on the trigger, not knowing why he was there or why he should or should not kill himself ("It simply seemed like a good idea at the time"). Paradoxically, though the addict is exhausted, sleep is fitful or impossible. Craving for cocaine may be quite low during this period.

Ends with: After two or three days of depression, mood begins to improve and addict enters Stage Three.

Stage Three: Honeymoon

Begins: Between one to six days after the last dose.

Signs & Symptoms: Euthymia (improved mood), moderate anxiety, restlessness, nervous tension; moderate but manageable craving; continued sleep disruption. In this stage, the addict concludes that the worst is over and typically vows to avoid cocaine in the future. "I'm not like those other fools," he tells himself. "I learn from experience." May decide he doesn't require professional treatment, because "I'm managing, aren't I?"

Ends with: Onset of Stage Four, and return of persistent, intense craving.

Stage Four: **Relapse Phase**

Begins: Typically, between six and fifteen days after last dose.

Signs & Symptoms: Craving returns, often in the form of vivid dreams, intrusive thoughts, and gradually increasing drug hunger. Defense mechanisms abound; the addict may find himself unable to recall the pain and depression of the recent crash. Paradoxically, his brain is flooded with remembered images of pleasurable early cocaine use.

Ends with: Unless the addict is involved in treatment, this stage normally results in relapse. Many cocaine addicts are on a two-week cycle. They binge for several days, crash for two or three more, feel better for a week or so, then begin to experience gradually worsening craving until some event (usually payday) provides them with the means to start the cycle all over again.

Stage Five: **Emotionalism**

Begins: Roughly fifteen to twenty-five days after the last use.

Signs & Symptoms: Emotional lability (fluctuation) is the hallmark of this stage. The addict is easily upset, prone to fits of temper, vulnerable to sudden attacks of remorse and depression. Each of these is enough to provoke relapse in the unwary. Ironically, the addict must also watch for strong, seemingly spontaneous sexual desires which are often directed toward another addict and which lead to the "bughouse romances" ("We met at the asylum") that plague treatment centers everywhere.

Ends with: This phase normally continues until the end of the first few months of abstinence, and is a principal reason why slogans such as "Easy Does It" and "One Day at a Time" are so popular in Twelve Step groups.

Stage Six: Conditioned Cues

Begins: Somewhere near the end of the first month of abstinence.

Signs & Symptoms: Craving strongly associated with settings or environments that remind the user of the cocaine experience. For example, seeing another drug user who is visibly intoxicated or in withdrawal; seeing someone with whom you've used drugs in the past; finding yourself in a setting which reminds you of drug use; seeing something which looks like drugs; a smell or sensation you associate with cocaine; the sight of money which in the past would have been used for a drug buy.

Ends with: This stage persists throughout much of the first year. Though not as intense as earlier stages, it has the advantage of catching the user unawares, producing strong cravings when he is least prepared to cope with them. This is the source of the Twelve Step warning against "slippery people and slippery places."

Of course, many addicts combine substances, so withdrawal profiles seldom unfold neatly. Remember, too, that there is great individual variance, with some heavy drinkers or drug users experiencing little withdrawal and others suffering very severe symptoms.

Both stimulant and depressant withdrawal often persist beyond the acute phase through what is commonly known as the *protracted withdrawal syndrome*. Characterized by the return of symptoms such as irritability, anxiety, craving, and insomnia for short episodes interspersed with longer periods of apparent good health, the protracted syndrome often undermines the recovering person's confidence in recovery and can, if not properly prepared for, provoke relapse.

PATHOLOGICAL ORGAN CHANGE

Alcohol and drug consumption damage the body in a variety of ways. Measurements of the extent of this damage can be used as diagnostic indicators of addiction, particularly with alcoholism. Sometimes the easiest way to ascertain whether or not someone is alcoholic is through the following lab tests:

GGT (Gamma Glutamyltransferase) is a liver enzyme which absorbs amino acids. Ranges above 40 units are usually associated with heavy drinking. GGT is useful in diagnosing alcoholism because it begins to elevate fairly quickly (after two to five drinks daily for a week) and returns to normal several weeks after drinking stops.

GGT can also be elevated by use of sedatives such as Valium or Xanax and antidepressants such as Elavil. If such factors are eliminated, however, GGT is about 90 percent accurate in identifying alcoholism. The GGT of hospitalized alcoholics often runs five to ten times higher than normal.

MCV (Mean Corpuscular Volume) is a measurement of the size of red blood cells. Heavy drinkers tend to have higher MCV results than others. To elevate your MCV to 80 or 90, you normally have to drink six to eight ounces of alcohol daily for five or six weeks. Short binges (a few days of heavy consumption) normally don't produce elevations.

An MCV of 98 or more almost always means severe alcoholism. Moreover, light or nondrinkers almost never show changes in MCV.

SGOT (aspartame transaminase) generally means enlarged fatty liver, a precursor of liver cirrhosis. Although heart disease and hepatitis can also elevate SGOT, it is believed to be 80 percent reliable as an indicator of alcoholism.

Alkaline Phosphatase is normally tested in conjunction with other liver function studies such as SGOT and GGT. It often confirms a diagnosis of alcoholic liver disease.

HDLC is a measure of high-density cholesterol and normally elevates with consumption of thirty to fifty grams of alcohol over about two weeks. Alcoholics show elevations about 90 percent of the time. This also returns to normal after two or three weeks of abstinence.

Uric acid levels do increase in heavy drinkers but aren't specific enough to stand alone as indicators of alcoholism. They are employed in conjunction with more reliable indicators such as MCV and GGT.

The best way to use the above tests is in combination. A study using both the GGT and the MCV correctly identified 91 percent of the alcoholics in a population of medical patients being treated under other diagnoses.

BEHAVIORAL SYMPTOMS

There are also a number of observable behaviors which allow us to differentiate the addict from the abuser.

COMPULSION

Addicts normally report that their desire to drink or use drugs may actually increase with continued use; this is known as the "potato chip syndrome" (one is too many, and a thousand is not enough). Compulsive disorders are normally treated with total abstinence from the compulsive behavior, because that is more easily achieved than moderation.

LOSS OF CONTROL

This behavior usually occurs with respect to the *amount consumed*, the *time and place* where drug use occurs, and the *duration* of a drinking or drugging episode.

For example, alcoholics frequently break vows to control their intake because of compulsion. Once they begin, they have trouble stopping. Something similar happens to the cocaine addict. One of our former patients made a deal with his supplier to sell crack in return for a small portion which he planned to keep for his own use. One night, however, he decided to smoke his share before going out to sell the rest. The drug's effects quickly wore off, leaving him craving more. He began to sample the crack he was supposed to sell, rationalizing that he would find wealthier customers who would pay a higher price. Before he realized the implications, all the crack was gone, and he was firmly in the area of deficit spending—only his creditor was a drug dealer rather than a bank.

LOSS OF CONTROL OVER TIME AND PLACE

This refers to the addict's tendency to use drugs in dangerous or inappropriate locations. One patient of ours used drugs regularly in her office—even going so far as to smoke crack at her desk. Another, a minor-league pitcher, hollowed out the handle of a bat, lined it with plastic, and filled it with vodka to be consumed in the bull pen. A police officer we treated was in the habit of carrying several packages of heroin in his uniform pocket and shooting up in the backseat of the patrol car. He was caught when he mistakenly reached in the wrong pocket for a cigarette and had to explain the balloon of dope which fell to the floor in front of his commanding officer.

Loss of control frequently results in what appears as blatantly self-destructive behavior. One prosecutor told the story of an offender who was facing three years in state prison for a serious drug charge. Through skillful negotiating, his attorney struck a deal with the prosecution that would allow the offender to serve the time in a drug program instead of prison. On the day of the sentencing, the prisoner appeared in the courtroom obviously under the influence of drugs, and to his lawyer's chagrin, the judge threw out the deal and sentenced the man to the full state prison term.

LOSS OF CONTROL OVER DURATION OF EPISODE

This is marked by the appearance of binges, extended periods of drug use where the addict may not eat or sleep except sporadically. Many addicts binge for several days at a time, some go for weeks or even months. Such binges often end in overdose or hospitalization, a spectacular gesture such as a suicide attempt, or an accident resulting in someone's death.

CONTINUED USE DESPITE ADVERSE CONSEQUENCES

One of the best ways to detect addiction is through the addict's tendency to return to drug use despite the problems it causes. For instance, the rate of alcoholism among second or third drunk-driving offenders is much greater than among first offenders. Likewise, the simplest way to identify alcoholics within a population of general hospital patients is to look for persons hospitalized more than once for several common alcohol-related diagnoses. The assumption is that persons with addictive disease do not respond to ordinary medical and behavioral interventions and therefore constitute the bulk of recidivists.

Examples abound. An addict was once nearly murdered by his drug dealer for failing to repay his debts. The experience so frightened him that he swore on his mother's soul never again to touch cocaine. But such vows are short-lived; less than twenty-four hours later he was caught trying to break into his dealer's apartment to steal cocaine.

Still another addict destroyed her nasal septum snorting cocaine and had to undergo expensive, painful surgical reconstruction. Appalled, she knew drastic action was necessary. But rather than giving up cocaine, she decided to switch to smoking. Within a year, she was more than $100,000 in debt, and in jail for embezzlement—but at least her nose was intact.

People unfamiliar with addiction often marvel at stories of addicts spending $500 or $1000 a day on drugs. But there is no ceiling on the amount of money that can be spent, and sooner or later, addicts lose everything they have. If an addict has a million dollars, you can rest assured that his drug use will cost two million. If he has no money at all, he will figure out a service he can render. It can be compared to a race with a staggered start: Though the runners line up at different marks, the finish line remains the same. The ultimate cost of alcoholism and drug dependence is everything, and then some.

ADDICTIVE DEFENSES

Of course, the major obstacle to the kind of self-diagnosis we discussed earlier are the many defenses with which the addiction is surrounded. Defense mechanisms are significantly different from the overt concealment we often expect from the alcoholic. Where the goal of a lie is to deceive others, the objective of psychological defenses is to protect oneself from painful awareness. We've all seen this among the bereaved when someone dies, or in those who have been told they have a fatal illness. The alcoholic's defenses are not much different. Let's review them in some detail.

WHAT IS DENIAL?

Denial refers to the alcoholic's inability to accurately perceive the extent or severity of his problem. Think of it as an "exclusionary" defense: Rather than actively rejecting the diagnosis, the alcoholic frequently fails even to admit the possibility. A caller to a late-night talk show once gave a description of extensive hallucinations that had come and gone over the preceding weeks, since he had "cut way back on my drinkin', to maybe three or four six-packs a day." When advised by the host to seek help immediately, the caller demurred. "It can't be the alcohol," he insisted, "because I used to drink twice that much, and I didn't have any hallucinations then."

Once again, denial is a normal human defense mechanism, and the addict's version is simply a drug-influenced exaggeration of a coping device used by millions.

WHAT IS RATIONALIZATION?

An addict may acknowledge problems in her life while attributing them to causes other than addiction, or pointing out what she imagines to be mitigating circumstances. One such drinker insisted her arrest for drunk driving be rescinded because "I've been drunker than that thousands of times, and nobody ever picked me up for DWI." Another blamed her arrest on an anesthetic administered at the dentist's office—five days earlier. A heroin addict admitted six years of daily use, but claimed he had used no drugs on the day of his arrest—as if that obviated the rest of his history. A sedative addict insisted her chronic insomnia justified the quintuple dose of sleeping pills she took every night—not to mention at mid-morning.

Rationalizations allow the user (and often, those around them) to focus on other problems while addiction worsens.

WHAT IS EXTERNALIZATION?

The externalizer blames his or her drug use on outside forces or circumstances. "If you had my problems," he or she insists, "you'd drink, too." An elderly alcoholic insists, "My wife died five years ago, and I can't get over it," ignoring the twenty years of heavy drinking that preceded her death and her dying wish that he stop. "My job is incredibly stressful, and I need alcohol to cope," claims the man put on probation for missing work.

Externalizing hides the fact that alcoholism and drug dependence are the principal *causes* of problems in the addict's life—and abstinence is the fastest, most effective way to reduce stress.

WHAT IS MINIMIZING?

The minimizer acts as though alcohol and drug use is unimportant, even irrelevant, and problems can be solved through a simple act of will.

"I know I messed up," he insists, "but I learned my lesson. It won't happen again." Or points out that, "You've had too much on occasion, haven't you?"

The assumption is that treatment isn't required because the problem simply isn't severe enough to merit it.

WHAT IS INTELLECTUALIZING?

Intellectualizers selectively focus on small, even picayune points of contention or dispute to distract from discussion of addiction. Intellectualizers debate meanings and semantics, while ignoring the obvious. "What precisely do you mean by 'alcoholic'?" he asks his doctor.

WHAT IS UNDOING?

Undoing is a "lesser" defense which reflects the addict's belief that certain positive behaviors "make up" for the problems caused by drug use, without acknowledging the addiction. "What do you mean I drink too much?" he rails at his children. "Who's putting you through college?" Or: "Look, I sent flowers, and I apologized. You'd think she'd forgive and forget."

This confuses family members. "Sometimes he's an absolute beast, and I'm ready to toss him out on his ear," one wept. "But the next day he's the nicest, warmest, most loving person in the world." That's because he's subconsciously trying to *undo* his previous behavior.

What Is Displacement?

Displacement is one of the most common defenses, and involves taking out one's frustrations on the nearest available target. Irritable from withdrawal, the alcoholic arrives home in a foul mood, criticizing his wife's every real and imagined flaw until she practically begs him to have a drink. His motto: *The best defense is a good offense*. This drives the family into an avoidance pattern—which leaves the alcoholic free to drink as he pleases, without monitoring or criticism.

What Is Projection?

Contrary to popular belief, projection has nothing to do with imagining future events. Instead, it is the tendency to project one's own hostile thoughts or feelings onto others. "My supervisor is out to get me fired," the alcoholic insists, but can't explain his reasoning. In reality, it is his own hostility toward his supervisor (and the authority he represents) which accounts for his feelings.

What Is Regression?

Sometimes the alcoholic or addict, frustrated by the demands of addiction or recovery, exhibits a childlike dependence and intolerance for frustration. This is frequently mistaken for a dependent personality disorder, but normally disappears with sobriety.

Regression may also be seen during the recovery process, however. A recovering alcoholic who deliberately gets drunk to express her dissatisfaction with some life event (a conflict with someone, or loneliness, for example) is exhibiting regressive, irrational behavior, because a binge won't win an argument or attract new friends. Thus, the "problem" which "caused" the relapse was really an excuse to drink again.

WHAT IS ACTIVE NEGATIVISM?

One defense involves a facade of complete hostility toward anything that interferes with drinking or drug use. "Okay, so it's gonna kill me," the addict yells at his parents. "You think I give a shit? I'd rather die than listen to you morons!" Or in the treatment center: "Look, I'm here because the judge made me come, but I think you people are a bunch of jerks and I have no intention of doing anything more than I absolutely have to."

The role of active negativism is to create conflict which obscures the real issues of addiction and recovery. Soon enough, the addict has made everyone around him or her so angry that the issue of alcoholism is forgotten among general criticism of his or her rotten attitude. Once the desired uproar has been created, the addict can justify separating from the family or leaving the treatment center—which he views as permission to return to drugs.

WHAT IS PASSIVE NEGATIVISM?

The passively negative alcoholic exhibits the same degree of resistance to change as the openly hostile addict, but does so in a hidden or *covert* fashion. Efforts toward change are undermined through sabotage, neglect, inattention, and avoidance. She flees or bursts into tears at the mention of alcoholism, so that the family becomes convinced she is too emotionally fragile to handle the truth. Once in treatment, she refuses to participate in discussions; claims she "doesn't understand" what's expected of her; "forgets" to read literature; and isolates in her room. The intent is to slide through the treatment experience without being impacted in any way.

A CONSPIRACY OF DENIAL

These same defenses are often encountered among family members as well as addicts themselves. Most children of alcoholics go through a long period of denial about parental alcoholism, even in the face of obvious evidence. Husbands and wives often rationalize or externalize the causes of drinking or drug use, even to the point of uprooting the whole family and moving to another city in the hopes of effecting a "geographical cure." Perhaps most common is minimizing. A woman admitted to us that her husband had nearly strangled her to death during a drunken argument the evening before, but insisted he "didn't mean it—the light was very poor in the bedroom, and I don't think he could see my face turning blue."

WHY ADDICTS CAN'T SEE THE OBVIOUS

These defenses form the basis of "comparing out," the addict's predilection for focusing on symptoms he or she *doesn't have* instead of those that have been identified. Mentioning an episode of drunkenness often brings this response: "Sure, but how about that vacation to Florida? I didn't get drunk once, did I?" The addict operates on the assumption that one cancels the other. In reality, progressive diseases normally feature periods of apparent "remission," followed by problems of increasing severity. It isn't necessary to have all the symptoms of a disease (be it alcoholism, cancer, or heart disease) to qualify for the diagnosis. The ones you haven't experienced arrive with the passage of time.

Such defenses also may be found in other chronic diseases. Heart patients frequently deny obvious symptoms of cardiac problems, even in the face of pressure from family members, until they suffer a massive attack. Breast cancer patients ignore lumps until their disease makes mastectomy treatment unavoidable. For many of us, the treatment is more frightening than the disease, and rationalizing or minimizing symptoms is a common way of protecting ourselves from painful anxiety.

We must never forget that alcoholism and drug addiction are

stigmatized illnesses, often wrongly attributed by otherwise intelligent people to moral perversity, weakness of will, social deprivation, and spiritual decay. This inhibits early recognition by addict
and family alike. Imagine that cancer was widely believed to be the
result of a hidden criminal nature. How many people would show
up for free cancer screenings? Stigma also creates what James
Milam calls the "third order symptoms" of shame and guilt which
the addict (even well into recovery) is encouraged to feel for actions
which were really the product of the disease. Such misplaced shame
also discourages early recognition. Despite the examples of recovering persons and the education of the past few decades, most Americans continue to see addiction more as crime than illness, accusation
than diagnosis. In this respect, we remain a long way from treating
addiction for what it really is.

THE BLACKOUT EXPERIENCE

One problem which complicates the task of self-diagnosis is flawed
recollections. Alcoholics and addicts frequently do not recall extensive portions of their addictive experience. Accordingly, the painful
events which are burnt into the memory cells of their loved ones
may produce little or no remorse in the drinker, because he or she
doesn't recall them. Donald Goodwin's research indicated that
about 50 percent of alcoholics report multiple "blackouts"—periods
of time when drinking which cannot be recalled when sober.

Blackouts appear to be a form of *state dependent learning*, similar
to that experienced by college students who used amphetamines to
cram for examinations in the 1960s, then often discovered to their
horror that once drug-free, they were no longer able to recall the
information learned while under the influence. The alcoholic is also
horrified to discover gaps in his memory of a drinking episode—
gaps that can range from several hours to days or even weeks.

No one knows precisely how blackouts work, but the following
model is helpful. Start with the assumption that every drinker has a
certain blood alcohol level beyond which he or she will experience a
blackout—what we call the *blackout point*. Most of us never have
blackouts because our blackout point is much higher than our
tolerance for alcohol, as illustrated in the following diagram.

BLACKOUT LEVEL AND NORMAL TOLERANCE

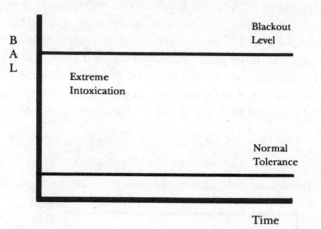

But suppose our tolerance is increasing (as does the alcoholic's) and we begin to drink past our blackout point. We discover that we are unable to recall all or part of a previous drinking episode— specifically, the portion where our blood alcohol was above the blackout point.

ALCOHOLIC EXCEEDING THE BLACKOUT PERIOD

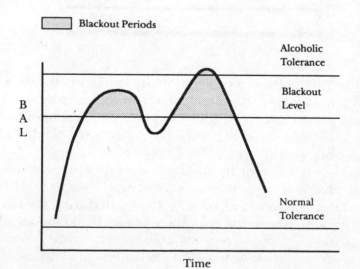

At first we "lose" only those portions of the evening where we were most intoxicated. We recall going to a party and having a good time, for instance, but can't remember how we got home. Eventually, however, we find ourselves unable to recollect whole evenings, as though our blackout point has lowered with the progression of alcoholism. Now, all drinking episodes are riddles with blackouts, and we find ourselves at a loss to account for our own behavior, reduced to making feeble excuses for things we don't recall having said or done.

LATER STAGE BLACKOUT PATTERN

Increase in blackouts as disease progresses

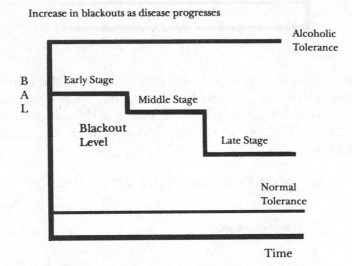

The blackout phenomenon alerts many families to the severity of an addictive problem. Mixing alcohol with other drugs is yet another way to increase the risk of blackouts. Synergistic substances such as tranquilizers or narcotics combined with alcohol almost guarantee blackouts.

A blackout is different from *short-term memory loss* which haunts many alcohol and drug users (see discussion on page 181). We assume the experiences recorded by the brain during the blackout episode are stored somewhere in the memory banks, because there are numerous reports of persons able to remember events from earlier blackouts when drunk. But these storage areas are apparently not accessible to the sober brain, and many recovering alcoholics claim no memory of much of their drinking career—up to and including crimes they may have committed.

ARE GAMBLING, COMPULSIVE SEXUAL ACTIVITY, AND EATING DISORDERS ALSO ADDICTIONS?

In recent years, the term addiction has been applied to a variety of compulsive disorders which don't involve drugs or alcohol. There are reasons for making this intellectual leap—but there are also many reasons for avoiding it.

Though gambling, compulsive sexual behavior, and morbid overeating indeed share many of the features of alcoholism and drug dependence—principally compulsion, loss of control, and continued use despite adverse consequences—they do not share the characteristic which from a biogenic perspective is the most important: chronic exposure to a chemical or toxin which spurs the body to adapt and lays the groundwork for the disease. Thus, it's quite possible (even, in the view of many scientists, *probable*) that these conditions spring from a quite different set of causes. Lumping together all disorders with compulsive features, therefore, is likely to create false assumptions about cause and effect, unwittingly reinforcing the discredited "psychogenic" paradigm—which holds that addiction is a response to the stress of psychosocial problems. Despite its popularity, there's no good evidence to support this paradigm, and plenty to contradict it.

Proponents of the psychogenic paradigm claim that people cite as evidence the observation that some recovering people renounce drinking or drugs only to turn to compulsive eating, gambling, or sexual behavior. Perhaps you know someone for whom this seemed to be true. Yet the vast majority of recovering addicts and alcoholics are neither overweight nor addicted to wagering and sex. Good adoption studies have been able to tease apart the predisposition for alcoholism from these other behaviors. When we see someone with both alcohol and gambling, food, or sexual problems, we should regard that as a true *dual diagnosis*. Both merit treatment, but we should not assume that one caused the other, or that they are two facets of the same underlying personality disorder.

Another example of the confusion of cause and effect concerns the co-existence of addiction and depressive disorders. Depression and alcoholism often run in the same families, and it is not uncommon to encounter individuals who suffer from both. Yet contrary to Freudian tenets, renouncing alcohol does not automatically produce a depressive reaction in the alcoholic. Researchers have found that after a reasonable period of recovery, the prevalence of symptoms of mental illness among recovering alcoholics is about the same as within the population as a whole. The residual depression associated with early recovery—probably the result of an unbalanced brain chemistry, a severely disrupted lifestyle, and often shame and guilt reinforced by misdirected therapy—abates over the first year or so of recovery. That is, unless the recovering person has enrolled in psychoanalytically oriented psychotherapy, and is led to conclude that he suffers from some chronic psychiatric illness. Once this occurs, the recovering person may spend years or even decades chasing a phantom "cause" for his or her lingering unhappiness. (But that's for yet another book.)

In the next chapter, we'll take a look at the mystery of relapse. Why do some alcoholics and addicts return to alcohol and drugs?

Chapter Seven

THE PARADOX OF RELAPSE

NONBELIEVERS ARE SKEPTICS, and if there's one thing that raises questions about the viability of treatment and recovery, it's the incidence of relapse. After all, the nonbeliever asks, why undertake something which may very well result in failure?

It's a good question, and one asked by every alcoholic and family, believer and nonbeliever alike. In fact, relapse is the single most misunderstood aspect of addiction. Because the average person doesn't grasp the true significance of relapse, he or she often wrongly concludes that treatment itself is futile. Because many professionals do not clearly understand the role of relapse in the recovery process, they frequently involve their recovering patients in expensive, insight-oriented psychotherapy which complicates the normal course of recovery (and ultimately fails to prevent relapse, anyway). Because family and loved ones misinterpret the causes or implication of relapse, they may respond with anger or punishment which ironically fosters still more relapses. And because the lawmakers who govern the world's nations do not appreciate the significance of relapse in terms of treatment outcome, they assume that treatment doesn't work and naively invest their country's resources in ill-designed prevention programs, or launch extended, costly, painful, and ultimately fruitless "wars" on addictive disease.

We're going to try to avoid some of these common errors, and instead look at relapse for what it is—a dangerous but entirely predictable obstacle in the treatment of addictive disease.

To begin, there are three key points to remember about the phenomenon of relapse.

1. **Relapse is a problem in the treatment of many diseases.** Think of recidivism as a problem inherent in medicine rather than peculiar to alcoholism. Recall that we have no cure for most common chronic disorders. In the absence of a cure, we are forced to rely on the patient's willingness to adhere to a regimen of treatment. Unfortunately, this regimen is often difficult and normally includes significant changes in long-established behavior.

Diabetics are asked to dramatically restrict their diets, monitor blood sugar several times daily, self administer injections and medications, maintain regular exercise, and resist gnawing cravings for sugar which are often *intensified* by insulin injections. Likewise, patients with coronary heart disease are expected to drastically limit their intake of salt, avoid fatty foods, participate in rehabilitative exercise programs, reduce their workload no matter what the demands of their occupation, take a variety of potent and sometimes dangerous medications exactly as prescribed. We would not describe either of these regimens as particularly enjoyable or convenient. Thus, diabetics and heart patients are under constant temptation to cheat, and to one extent or another, *nearly all of them do*. As a result, many suffer frightening, painful, or even life-threatening recurrences of acute illness. These are the equivalent of alcoholic relapses, and they are the bane of physicians everywhere.

2. **The relapser often has little or no insight into the causes of a particular relapse.** Though relapsers often provide an "explanation" for their return to drinking or drug use, it may not reflect the actual circumstances that produced a given relapse. That's because addicts are blinded by the same defense mechanisms—denial, rationalization, externalization, minimizing, intellectualizing, etc.—that prevented them from seeing the severity of their addiction for years before they arrived in treatment. Thus, relapse is often blamed on psychological or social problems which may in fact have

little or nothing to do with the decision to return to alcohol or drugs. Meanwhile, the real etiology of that particular relapse remains a mystery to the relapser. This undermines the effort to prevent subsequent relapses and is a primary reason so many addicts fall into a cycle of repeated drinking episodes.

3. **Relapse does not necessarily indicate treatment failure.** People unfamiliar with addiction (we include nearly everyone in the media) commonly take relapse as a sign that treatment has failed. There's no objective reason to draw that conclusion. Many relapsers terminate drinking or drug use and go on to become models of sobriety. Most of the founders of groups like Alcoholics Anonymous, for example, had long histories of relapse and aborted attempts at sobriety prior to their success in the Twelve Step program. Groups such as Secular Sobriety, Rational Recovery, and Women for Sobriety sprang into existence because their early members were unsuccessful in other programs. Remember, new self-help groups and schools of therapy appear precisely because people are not reaching their goals elsewhere, and strive to learn from their mistakes.

PREDICTABLE PROBLEMS IN RECOVERY

Addicts (and often others, as well) unconsciously expect that removal of alcohol and drugs means an instantaneous end to most if not all of their many problems. If you're a nonbeliever looking for a way to exercise your skepticism, you might reject abstinence when you don't find immediate serenity. But a central nervous system damaged by months or years of assault with massive doses of alcohol and drugs refuses to heal overnight. The life problems associated with the addicted lifestyle don't disappear with the last drink. Despite the vast improvement in judgment and coping ability which accompanies sobriety, the first year or two of recovery remains fraught with problems. An alcoholic who has not been properly prepared for such difficulties will often "give up" and return to drinking.

Good treatment takes responsibility for preparing the newly sober person for the realities of initial sobriety, regardless of spiritual beliefs. It's part of equipping yourself for life without alcohol and drugs.

Here are some common problems in early recovery, with suggestions for dealing with them should they occur.

PERSISTENT CRAVINGS

Craving is a normal response to deprivation of something the brain has been conditioned to expect—such as a drug. Since the body operates on the principle of *homeostasis* (internal balance and stability), the brain constantly monitors its own systems for signs of a surfeit or deficit of key chemicals. Once the body learns that heroin, cocaine, or alcohol quickly rectifies such deficits, it signals for them via cravings. If the drug is supplied, the craving instantly disappears—only to return later, often in greater intensity.

Don't get the idea that this is confined to addicts and alcoholics. Anyone who has ever been on a restrictive diet is thoroughly familiar with the phenomenon of craving. The more intense the deprivation, the stronger the brain's message to correct it. Of course, there's a catch-22 situation here as well. Satisfying a craving normally leads to more intense cravings within a few hours.

Let's illustrate this with a simplified model of the process of neurotransmission which can be used to explain how drugs hypothetically reinforce their own use. Figure 7-1 illustrates a *synapse*, a location in the brain where two nerve cells can communicate with one another. Note the "storage compartment" called a vesicle near the tip of Cell #1, filled with the neurochemical dopamine, thought to play an important role in the pleasure associated with cocaine use. Normally, when you engage in an activity which is pleasurable (sex, eating, etc.), your brain releases dopamine (among other chemicals) which in turn crosses the synapse to attach itself to Cell #2 at a location called a *receptor site*. This process, repeated at hundreds of thousands of synapses, produces the sensation you experience as pleasure.

That completed, the pleasure response has fulfilled its purpose, which is to reinforce certain types of behavior. The dopamine

FIGURE 7-1
NEUROTRANSMISSION AT THE SYNAPSE

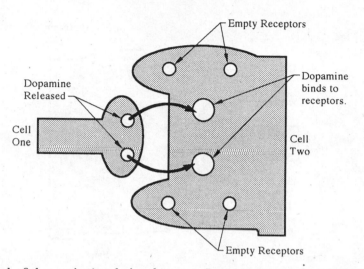

Model of dopamine's role in pleasure: In response to electrical stimulation of Cell #1, the vesicles release dopamine which crosses the synaptic cleft and binds to the receptors on Cell #2, stimulating more electrical activity.

detaches from the receptor and waits in the synapse to be reabsorbed by Cell #1, perhaps for further use.

That, greatly simplified, is how many scientists believe pleasure occurs. Now suppose you've ingested cocaine, and the cocaine finds its way to these same synapses (see figure 7-2 on page 172). When dopamine is released, the cocaine theoretically binds to the storage compartment on Cell #1, so that it can't reabsorb the free dopamine. That's called *blocking re-uptake*. If it isn't reabsorbed, the dopamine levels in the brain remain unusually high for a brief period, contributing to a general feeling of *euphoria* (extreme feelings of pleasure independent of the environment). After a while, however, the dopamine is eliminated. When the cocaine finally detaches from Cell #1 and is washed away, the situation in the synapse returns to normal—except that this particular synapse has lost some of its precious dopamine in the process.

FIGURE 7-2
COCAINE AND DOPAMINE IN THE SYNAPSE

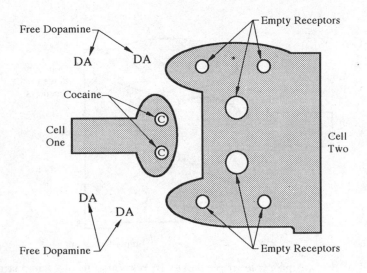

If this occurs often enough in dopamine-rich areas of the brain, you can actually develop a *dopamine deficit syndrome,* meaning your brain suffers a chronic shortage of this key substance. That can affect your mood and your thinking processes, for the worst. The homeostatic mechanisms of the brain, struggling to compensate for your cocaine-induced dopamine deficit, may send nearly constant cravings as a signal to provide yet more cocaine. But if you give into them, you will discover yourself with still greater deficits in the near future.

Craving also comes in a number of different forms. The following are some examples:

The Drug Dream: You begin to have nightmares (or even daymares, on occasion) about drinking or drug use. These visions may be so real that you might actually feel you have experienced a relapse.

The Intrusive Thought: While attempting to concentrate on something else, you find yourself distracted by persistent images of drug use. "I can't seem to get it out of my head," you complain, wondering how you'll ever remain abstinent in the face of such continuing psychological pressure.

The Selective Memory: You find yourself unable to clearly recall the negative aspects of a recent drug episode, as if your brain insists on remembering only those parts which reinforce further drug use. Even a painful or embarrassing memory fades quickly to be replaced by fond recollections of the earliest days of drug use, when drugs were fun and problems few.

Plotting: You find yourself imagining scenarios in which you could drink or use drugs without getting in trouble. "Maybe if I gave the car keys to the bartender," you think, "and told him not to give them to me no matter how much I begged or threatened him ... then even if I did go into a blackout, I wouldn't be able to get another drunk-driving arrest."

Severe Drug Hunger: Occasionally during its struggle to rebalance its neurochemistry, the brain will send cravings so intense they resemble the first stages of withdrawal. You find yourself trembling, unable to eat or sleep, sure that only more cocaine or heroin will restore you to sanity.

As a recovering person, however, you have one enormous advantage in the war against craving: it goes away by itself. In fact, severe cravings seldom last more than ten or fifteen minutes. If you can distract yourself, or use a relaxation exercise, or find someone to reassure you, craving is quite harmless. It's only when you give in and return to drugs that craving worsens. Remember, you suffer from a disease characterized by compulsion: Small amounts of a drug don't satisfy, they simply increase the body's demand for more. If you don't give in, however, the body eventually adjusts to life without the drug, and further cravings are few and far between.

An Exercise for Dealing with Craving

Here's a simple technique for learning to cope with the intrusive thoughts and feelings that characterize drug hunger. Find a comfortable chair and sit with your feet flat on the floor and your hands palm down on your thighs (remove your shoes if you like). Allow your eyes to close and then picture in your "mind's eye" a television screen like the one in your own home. The screen should be blank. Now, picture your craving on the screen, as an object. Use whatever shape, size, and color seems "right" to you. Stare at it for a moment. Is the shape moving or still? Does it stay the same color or shift in shade? Just let it sit on the screen—make no effort to change it, or to get away from it. It's no longer "inside you"—it's now projected onto the screen, where you can view it like anything else on television.

Got it? Now, visualize a remote control in your hand—a channel changer. Picture yourself holding the control up so you can see the various buttons. Find the one that says "Channel." See it? Now, press that button. As you do, you hear a small click from the television set. When you look up, you're looking at a different channel. It's a scene of a tranquil, beautiful beach—white sand, beautiful water, warm sun, gentle breeze. Imagine yourself on that beach, relaxing, thinking about nothing in particular, enjoying life. When you feel good again, open your eyes and go do something you enjoy.

After a while, you'll be able to simply visualize the craving on your mental TV set, switch the channel to the beach scene, and go back to whatever you were doing.

EMOTIONALISM

Early recovery is also characterized by heightened emotional responses. Milam calls this *emotional augmentation.* The nervous system of the newly sober alcoholic or addict augments his or her emotions to produce an overreaction to everyday problems, akin to what occurs when someone is under extraordinary stress. Even if you're ordinarily the most rational person around, initial sobriety will probably leave you temporarily susceptible to mood swings and surprising outbursts. This may seem particularly disquieting to the nonbeliever who usually displays tremendous control over her emotions.

Once again, consider the problem from a biological perspective.

Our feelings—ranging all the way from motherly love to the tangle of sensations roiling in our "gut"—actually originate in an area of the brain known as the *limbic system.* For years, this region was largely ignored by brain researchers, dismissed as the "rhinoencephalon" and noted only for its relationship to our sense of smell. But in the 1930s, a series of experiments involving the stimulation and/or removal of various structures within the rhinoencephalon of laboratory animals revealed a remarkable range of effects on the animal's behavior. By turns, a monkey could be made to attack in homicidal rage, withdraw into abject fear, masturbate compulsively, even lose or gain appetite for food, simply as a result of selective manipulation of brain centers by the experimenter. The humble rhinoencephalon was renamed the limbic system (from the Greek *limbus,* meaning "ring") and identified as having a primary role in governing our emotional responses.

Four human behaviors were thought to be heavily influenced by activity in the limbic system. The first was anger—the emotion associated with self defense and the perception of external threat. The second was fear, the most primitive of feelings and the one most directly connected to survival. These two behaviors, taken together, form the basis for the "fight/flight" response which is the animal kingdom's response to danger.

Feeding was yet another behavior believed to be dominated by limbic activity. Emotions directly affect appetite, as anyone who has been on a very restrictive diet can attest. The last behavior associated with the limbic system was of course mating, or sex drive. We probably don't have to explain the all-important role of emotions in sex.

One result of limbic system research was the inescapable conclusion that emotions could be dramatically affected not only by external stimuli but by alterations in the chemistry of the brain itself. Simple stimulation with electrical current in the appropriate region was enough to send the subject into paroxysmal rage or catatonic withdrawal. What, then, was the impact on emotions of large doses of alcohol, LSD, or heroin? Or of the process of addiction, with its extremes of tolerance and physical dependence?

Milam compared the brain of the alcoholic in withdrawal to that of the animal stimulated by electricity. Each external stimulus—an argument with the spouse, frustration with the boss, depression over a financial setback—is influenced by withdrawal-related agitation in the limbic system. The addict, unaware of this process of augmentation, naturally attributes the intensity of his emotions to the severity of the stimulus. "I'm so angry because my wife is so unfair," he concludes. "Anybody would feel the same way in my situation." It never occurs to him that the alcohol or drugs he consumed the night before was still influencing his behavior, even though he considered himself "sober." One cocaine user loudly insisted that he was never irritable following a crack binge. "I'm perfectly calm the next morning," he claimed. "Just last Monday, I was twenty minutes late to work, and my supervisor asked me why. Sure, I wanted to hit him, but I didn't."

Augmented emotions poison relationships. Just as the alcoholic fails to appreciate the influence of toxicity on his emotions, so, too, do his family and friends. They assume that the angry, frightened, or depressed individual they see in front of their eyes is the "real" you. "He's a completely different person than he used to be," they tell their friends and therapists. "Almost anything will set him off. I'm afraid even to talk around him anymore."

Withdrawal persists in its post-acute phase well into recovery, and the process of emotional augmentation is a major obstacle to early recovery. The newly sober alcoholic may react with rage or depression to even minor frustrations. If you want to see augmentation in action, spend some time volunteering in a nonmedical detox unit. You'll see extreme responses to the most minor provocations.

There is a paradox here: Though the alcoholic tends to overrespond to small difficulties, this same augmented nervous system sometimes goes into its version of "shock" when confronted with a legitimate catastrophe. News of a death in the family may be met with what seems to be flat, uncaring acceptance—except for the real emotional storms which follow days or weeks later.

Most of your experience of the initial months of abstinence is dominated by your struggle to cope with your own intensified feelings. For a nonbeliever who places a high value on reason, this can be quite disconcerting and confusing. Passion and irrationality replace logic. This new world can be frightening. But don't let it keep you from seeking help from others. Whether you involve yourself in a Twelve Step group, Secular Sobriety, Rational Recovery, psychotherapy, or any combination of the above, you'll find much of the discussion devoted to the need to learn to maintain rational perspective in the face of sometimes volcanic emotions.

An Exercise for Dealing with Intense Emotions

It's helpful to record this into a tape recorder and play it back as a guide for this particular experience. As you read into the microphone, speak clearly but slowly, allowing time for each part of the process.

Once again, find a quiet place, dim the lights, placing your feet flat on the floor and hands palm down on your thighs. Now concentrate on your breathing. Imagine that as you inhale deeply, a warm, golden fluid enters your body, soothing and relaxing as it flows into your chest. It feels wonderful. As you exhale deeply, you push the fluid further into your body: first into your stomach, where it relaxes the tension there. Then into your arms and legs, where it smoothes the knotted muscles so you feel yourself seeming to sink into the chair. Feel the fluid massage the joints of your wrists and hands, your ankles and feet. Perhaps they're tingling. When the fluid is flowing through your limbs, allow some to flow upward into your shoulders and neck, warming and relaxing as it goes. With each breath, you feel more relaxed. Let the fluid flow from your neck into your face, warming and relaxing, massaging the area behind your eyes, smoothing the muscles of your jaw and forehead.

When all the regions of the body are relaxed, allow the fluid to flow smoothly out of your body with each exhalation. You feel warm and relaxed. Count to three, and open your eyes. Now, do something you enjoy.

After you become accustomed to this technique, you'll be able to call up the golden fluid at any time, and benefit immediately from the warmth and relaxation it brings.

SLEEP DISRUPTION

Although many recovering people sleep normally, another common complication of sobriety is "fractured" or disrupted sleep. There are a number of variations: You may have trouble getting to sleep, suffering from frequent awakenings, find yourself awake and unable to return to sleep after only a few hours of rest, or discover yourself afflicted with horrific nightmares.

Sleep is one of the most fragile of human behaviors. Most of us experience sleep disruption at one time or another, for a variety of reasons: anxiety, tension, excess caffeine consumption, distracting aches and pains. Many scientists believe that the addict's persistent difficulties with sleep spring from alcohol and drug-induced deficits in *serotonin*. These deficits are hard to correct. Normal diet doesn't contain enough serotonin precursors (such as those found in warm milk, a traditional sleep aid) to ensure a return to normal sleep. Thus, some otherwise healthy and well-nourished recovering persons experience sleep problems years after their last drink.

There is no panacea for sleep problems. Sleeping pills, mostly of the cross-addictive benzodiazepine family, can reawaken the craving for alcohol or other drugs. Besides, they are not effective for long-term use. If your sleep difficulties are persistent and pronounced, you may want to contact your local hospital or sleep disorders clinic for a *sleep study*, in which your rest is observed and monitored by experts. Such studies often identify problems such as *sleep apnea* (periods where breathing stops) which can be corrected with breathing aids.

Even if you can't guarantee a full night's rest, you can learn some techniques to help you go back to sleep. Most of these are based on an understanding of the *Reticular Activating System* (RAS)—the brain's arousal mechanism.

The RAS has a number of responsibilities. First, it keeps you awake. Second, it appears to play a key role in screening out stimuli which might otherwise distract you from concentrating on your work, or from resting peacefully. The RAS is programmed to call your attention to new or potentially dangerous stimuli in your environment. For example, if someone familiar walks into the room at this very moment, your attention will be drawn to their entrance, but once they have been identified, you will quickly return your focus to your reading. That's the RAS at work. But suppose the newcomer was wearing a stocking mask and carrying an Uzi? The brain would refuse to permit you to ignore it. The RAS would continue to call your attention to the stranger until you had removed the threat of danger.

It should be easy to make the connection between the danger-sensing mechanisms of the RAS and the heightened emotions of the newly sober alcoholic. Thinking about your problems while lying in bed, for instance, will almost invariably mean a sleepless night. A dream about an anxiety provoking situation will produce rapid awakening. The RAS doesn't distinguish real from imagined dangers. It wakes you up for all of them.

Thus, you may need to develop some techniques for putting yourself back to sleep, by distracting the RAS.

An Exercise for Going to Sleep

Lie on your back in bed, with the lights out or dimmed. If it's more comfortable, put an extra pillow under your knees. Take several deep breaths, making sure to exhale deeply before taking new air into your lungs.

Now, imagine yourself lying comfortably on the sand at the beach. It's a warm day, clear skies, a few clouds scattered about. There's a gentle breeze that makes the temperature perfect. You're quite relaxed—you don't have a care in the world.

If you like, imagine yourself sitting up and looking all around you. First to the left—see anything? Then the right. Look straight ahead at the horizon, over the perfect blue expanse of ocean. The waves are small and friendly-looking. The sand is unblemished.

Now lay back on the beach and close your eyes. Breathe easily and gently. You feel yourself getting sleepy, and you simply follow along. Just breathe. Just breathe.

Do this every night when you go to bed, and whenever you wake up during the night. You don't need to make any conscious effort to go to sleep. It will simply happen. You won't even notice when it does.

WEIGHT GAIN OR LOSS

Most people gain or lose weight when they give up alcohol and drugs. This is probably related to not one but three physiological processes. First is the alteration in food metabolism which occurs as the body readjusts to life without stimulants and depressants. Second is presence of food cravings (perhaps for sweet or salty foods) which are often high in fat content.

Though almost everyone gains or loses seven to ten pounds during the first year of abstinence, a small percentage of recovering persons will experience dramatic increase or decrease in weight, often related to compulsive overeating or bulimia. If you have a history of eating disorders or see the signs reflected in weight fluctuation, consult a physician or specialist in eating problems.

Make an effort to avoid "sugar cycles"—binges on foods high in sugar or fats which trigger dramatic peaks and valleys in blood sugar. Authors Katherine Ketcham and L. Ann Mueller, in their book *Eating Right to Live Sober*, recommend approximating a hypoglycemic (low blood sugar) diet, eating six small meals daily to level out fluctuations in blood glucose. Avoid candies and other sweets, which make you feel better temporarily but lead to even more drastic dips in glucose.

Something else to avoid: quick weight-loss plans. A general rule: The faster you take off weight (especially if you do it on a starvation diet), the unhealthier the effects on your recovering physiology, and the faster you'll gain it back once you start eating again. It really is better to eat conservatively and lose half a pound a week than to go on a crash diet and lose ten pounds in ten days. If you remember the principle of homeostasis, you'll understand why. The body interprets the dramatic reduction in food intake as the result of some environmental crisis (for example, you're stranded in the woods without anything to eat). It compensates by slowing your metabolism to a crawl, stopping weight loss almost entirely, and also by sending you strong persistent cravings for various foods. You'll find yourself engaged in a war with your own body— and you will ultimately lose. In this particular war, losing means gaining back all the weight you took off, plus an extra five to twenty pounds.

So go slow, and seek a doctor's supervision before you start. It's worth the time and effort.

FORGETFULNESS

Another vulnerable brain function is memory. The process of remembering something actually involves three linked processes: immediate retention, short-term post-distractional memory, and long-term recollection. *Immediate retention* is your ability to recall information you just received. As an experiment, study the following sequence of numbers:

21791

Now, without looking at the page, repeat the numbers out loud. Were you able to do it without error? All right, try the next sequence:

498243

Once again, repeat it out loud without cheating. If you were successful, try the following sets:

3987685
51839263
208391769

Most people can handle six or seven digits but have trouble with larger numbers. Even if you're recovering from alcoholism, you should have no trouble recalling four or five digit sequences.

Now let's test your *short-term memory*, or ability to recall something after an intervening period when you were thinking about something else. Write out in the space provided on the opposite page exactly what you had to eat yesterday. Include snacks and beverages.

Breakfast

Lunch

Dinner

Snacks

When you're finished, try doing the same thing for the day before yesterday.

Finished? Was that at all difficult? Maybe you just don't pay much attention to what you eat. Still, most recovering people report at least some problems with this exercise. Short-term memory deficits cause problems in learning-intensive settings like school or work. The solution: learn to take very complete notes, or to record meetings or conversations for later reference. Don't rely on your memory.

Long-term recollection is simply your ability to recall events or information you no longer use. Drinking and drug use don't seem to affect this process.

FATIGUE AND FLUCTUATIONS IN ENERGY

Some newly sober people become bundles of energy—so much so that they have trouble figuring out how to use all of it. Others experience chronic lethargy and fatigue. The majority, however, probably find themselves cycling between the two.

Once again, science is not certain what causes this. Extreme fatigue is often associated with depression, and some alcoholics are mistakenly diagnosed as clinically depressed entirely on the basis of this symptom. By the same token, episodes of high activity are often misidentified as symptoms of mania. Unless there are clearly identifiable symptoms of mood disorders such as bipolarity, it's likely that dramatic fluctuations are linked to sobriety rather than an underlying psychiatric illness.

It takes a while for the recovering person to adjust to his or her own fluctuating energy level. Our recommendation: During the active cycle, make a conscious effort to avoid overwork. Periodically stop to meditate or do a relaxation exercise. Deliberately leave some projects unfinished in favor of relaxing or socializing. The same applies to the "down" periods which follow: Make yourself get some mild exercise, get out of the house, spend time with people. Though therapists normally recommend you "go with the flow," the goal here is to lessen the peaks and valleys in activity, making sure the brain receives both the stimulation and the rest it needs during your periods of restlessness or inactivity. And avoid stimulants like caffeine—it will just make you irritable.

SEXUAL ADJUSTMENT

The last of our common problems in recovery has to do with one of the most delicate of human functions: sex. If you remember the oft-repeated credo of the sex therapist, that the body's true sex organ is the brain rather than the genitals, you'll see the reason this area is so often affected during the recovery process. Again, many sober people have no problems at all, while others run into unforeseen obstacles.

Sexual dysfunction comes in a number of forms. Some experience loss of interest or desire. Others have difficulty achieving orgasm or excitement. Still others find themselves with a surfeit of sexual desire. Whatever the problem, there's a good chance it is directly or indirectly related to your rebalancing hormones.

Cocaine, for example, achieves some of its euphoric effects by robbing the brain of many of the same neurochemicals which make sex pleasurable. That's why people so often compare cocaine intoxication to orgasm, and also an explanation for the increased libido experienced by many novice users. But we also know that many (if not most) cocaine addicts eventually develop signs of sexual disorders, up to and including impotence in males and inorgasmia in females. Clearly, cocaine use has in some way depleted the body's ability to produce adequate amounts of sex-related neurochemicals. When cocaine use stops, the body begins to replenish these deficits. But who is to say how long this process takes?

It's easy to see problems in this area could spur the emotionally augmented alcoholic to relapse. Our advice: Be patient with recovery. If problems occur, discuss them with someone knowledgeable. If you're worried that your sexual difficulties are caused by something other than the residual effects of your addiction, visit a specialist. Depending on the problem, that might mean an assessment by a physician at an impotence clinic or by a mental health professional at a sexual dysfunction counseling program. Good treatments exist, and we can assure you that no matter what the problem, you will eventually find a solution—provided you avoid a return to alcohol or drugs. Just approach each problem rationally, and continue to maintain your faith in recovery.

THE MEANING OF RELAPSE

Relapse, as we explained earlier, is not really a very good indicator of ultimate treatment failure. Many persons who experience relapse *eventually* go on to establish stable sobriety. Here's an example from our clinical casebook. The names and occupation have been changed, of course, but the dynamics of relapse are quite typical. As you read, note the various rationalizations the addict uses to justify his failure to treat his disease.

WHIRLYBIRD WASHINGTON AND THE OCCASIONAL BEER

Delvin "Whirlybird" Washington was the best jumper in college basketball. Though only six feet tall, Delvin had been told his future in the professional leagues was bright. With any luck, he would be a millionaire at twenty-five.

Delvin rarely exerted himself scholastically. As early as junior high, he could persuade his teachers to push him through from one grade to the next, claiming the only reason his marks were so low was that he spent so much time playing basketball, the one activity he was truly passionate about. After all, he would tell them, his constant workouts made him into the hero of the team, and brought glory to his school. If left to his own devices, the teachers would hear, Delvin would build himself into superstar material—a top professional athlete who would make everyone proud of him.

Delvin's fondness for cocaine began in high school. In his neighborhood, cocaine wasn't considered a dangerous drug like PCP or heroin. But the phenomenal self-discipline Delvin brought to sports didn't seem to carry over to experiments with drugs. By his final year of college, he found himself on periodic two- or three-day binges, stopping only when he ran out of cocaine and money. He was even starting to consider shaving points as a way of paying off some of his debts to the people who once upon a time had been only too happy to supply him with free cocaine.

As far as he was concerned, there was no reason to give up coke—the pleasure he got from it didn't seem to be standing in the way of his basketball. But eventually, Delvin was caught on a routine urine test, when the teammate from whom he normally borrowed a clean sample failed to show up for practice. The university suspended Delvin from the squad and insisted that he enter a twenty-eight day rehab program.

To his surprise, Delvin actually liked treatment. Bolstered by the atmosphere of sobriety and good fellowship, Delvin realized that cocaine was going to cost him a very lucrative basketball career, and swore never to use it again. He was sure that cocaine made him into a completely different person—one who was weak-willed and irresponsible. He thanked God for getting him out of trouble, and was confident he could get his life back to normal in no time.

The day he got out, Delvin wanted to set things straight with his teammates. He took several of them out to dinner and told them all about his addiction and how he planned never to use drugs again.

"Yeah, but should you be drinking that beer, then?" one of them asked, pointing at the pitcher Delvin had ordered.

"Why not?" Delvin replied. "Never had no problem with beer."

"Yeah," said another teammate. "Beer ain't a drug. Beer is a sponsor."

Three hours after dinner, Delvin found himself on a street corner in the ghetto, trying to find somebody who would sell him some crack. Unfortunately, the dealer he selected was an undercover cop, and Delvin was taken to jail.

His basketball career in ruins, worried that he would be sent to state prison, Delvin was only too happy to accept the judge's order that he be remanded to a six-month residential drug program. Once again, he did well in confinement, but relapsed less than sixty days after he moved back in to his apartment. He couldn't understand what drove him back to cocaine. Delvin still attended counseling sessions, avoided all his friends from the old neighborhood, and never drank anything stronger than a glass of wine. What could be more innocent?

Over the following twelve months, Delvin experienced three more relapses. In each case, the situation was the same. Delvin would go to a party, drink a few beers, say goodnight to everyone, go home, and wake up a few hours later with an irresistible urge for cocaine. After three or four days of binging which left him broke, depressed, and sometimes suicidal, Delvin would sign himself into a detox unit. His basketball career was a shambles, and Delvin was beginning to doubt whether he would ever amount to anything. He blamed everyone for his problems, especially God, who had inexplicably turned from him. It wasn't until someone at a meeting mentioned the importance of giving up alcohol that Delvin began to question the role of drinking in his cocaine relapses.

"But I'm not an alcoholic," he protested to the speaker after the meeting had ended. "I never crave it, never have more than a couple, never get drunk."

"So what?" the speaker said. "You keep going back to coke."

"Not always. Nine out of ten times I'm out drinking, I just go right home to bed."

"But the tenth time, you don't."

This conversation had a big impact on Delvin. He'd heard something similar from his counselors, but had never paid much attention. "I don't want to give up drinking," he told himself, "but I'll try it for a while, and see if it helps."

Though Delvin had a number of problems during the ensuing months, including a bankruptcy and painful divorce, he remained abstinent and within three years was signed to a lucrative contract with a team in Europe.

Note how long it took Delvin to make the connection between drinking and relapse. That's because he was blinded by three factors:

1. **He did not regard himself as an alcoholic.** Though Delvin readily identified himself as a cocaine addict, he believed that his use of alcohol was entirely "social" and nonaddictive. This is a common mistake. Can the use of a mood-altering drug by a person with an extensive history of addiction to such drugs ever be regarded as entirely innocuous? Of course not. Whether or not Delvin met the clinical criteria for alcohol dependence, he was certainly vulnerable to relapse from other drugs. In fact, many addicts make exactly the same mistake with marijuana or a sleeping pill rather than alcohol.

2. **He was fooled by apparently "safe" drinking.** Like many addicts, Delvin mistook periods of control as evidence that his drinking was nonaddictive. In reality, most alcoholics experience progressive loss of control as a gradual process, with binges interspersed with apparently "normal" consumption. We may assume that as time passed, binges would become longer and more painful, and episodes of "safe" consumption few and far between.

We call such mistakes in interpretation and approach *cognitive errors.* Delvin's inaccurate or incomplete understanding of the disease led him to make decisions which undermined his sobriety and promoted relapse—despite his efforts to avoid it. It wasn't until Delvin recognized his error that he was able to change his behavior and avoid further binges.

In many instances, relapse is simply evidence of a slow learning curve—the newly sober person, struggling to cope with the unfamiliar limitations imposed by the disease, is learning from painful experience rather than textbooks. Delvin assumes that drinking is okay because he doesn't fit his conception of an alcoholic and because he often drinks without returning to cocaine. His assumption is incorrect, but it takes him a while to believe that. Though his counselors had advised him from the beginning to avoid alcohol, Delvin, like most addicts, insisted on learning the hard way.

This phenomenon distorts the statistics used to calculate "recovery rates" of various treatment programs. Such statistics are based on the presumption that effective treatment is effective immediately, and that an addict who relapses is always a "treatment failure." But suppose the alcoholic relapses after outpatient treatment A and inpatient treatment B and then establishes stable sobriety following yet a third treatment? Does that automatically mean that C was a success while A and B were a waste of time and money? Of course not, especially since most of attitude and behavior change upon which eventual sobriety was based probably occurred during treatment A and B. In fact, treatments A, B, and C may well have taken place within the same institution. We wish it weren't the case, but for many patients, the lessons of treatment are *cumulative*.

THE HIDDEN CAUSES OF RELAPSE

One of the best results of careful self-examination is that it allows you to isolate the deeply rooted behaviors and tendencies that will support your disease. Let's look at some other common mistakes in attitude and approach which normally result in a return to alcohol or drugs.

Cheating on Your Regimen

Maintaining recovery, especially in the initial months, requires that you place recovery-related activities above other priorities.

Case Illustration: Frank, age twenty-two, agreed to a schedule of outpatient counseling twice weekly following discharge from an inpatient program. But he quickly ran into scheduling problems. Frank had a lot of outstanding debts, and he jumped at the chance to work extra hours, which unfortunately conflicted with his outpatient appointments. After Frank had missed two of his first six sessions, his counselor asked for a meeting.

"Frank, you're not living up to your agreement," the counselor said.

"Sure I am," Frank insisted. "The only sessions I miss are ones that conflict with work. You can't expect me to ignore my job. I'll get fired."

"What if you use drugs again, and we pick it up on a urine test?" the counselor asked.

"I have no desire to do drugs," Frank said. "Besides, working the extra hours helps my sobriety. It keeps me busy and I'm paying off my bills. I thought that's what I was supposed to be doing."

Five weeks later, Frank called to terminate his involvement in outpatient care, informing the counselor that he felt he no longer needed it, and he had an opportunity to become a supervisor if he could impress the boss by working extra hard. Approximately ninety days after that discussion, Frank was fired by his boss for insubordination. Admitted to detox the following year, Frank complained bitterly about his former employer's "working me to death."

Cognitive Error: Frank assumes that he can maintain sobriety without working at it. Though he is indeed involved in productive, non-drug related activity, it is not a viable substitute for a recovery program. The pattern of overwork which he claims "keeps him busy" ultimately becomes the stress he blames for his eventual relapse. In reality, Frank's stress was self-induced.

To avoid this error: Set a personal goal of establishing a workable recovery program and then maintaining it in the face of other priorities. When your counselor gives you a direction, *follow it*, even if you don't immediately grasp its importance.

No Self-Diagnosis

Some addicts complete treatment without recognizing their disease. They ignore Step One's admission of powerlessness over alcohol or drugs. Without the spur of self-diagnosis, their motivation for continued sobriety drains away as the weeks pass.

Case Illustration: Nell, age thirty-one, entered outpatient treatment at the insistence of her husband. He was ready to file for divorce. Though she readily acknowledged that she drank excessively, she resisted the suggestion that she suffered from alcoholism.

"In the first place," she told her psychiatrist, "I didn't get drunk every day. There were days when I drank hardly at all. I never had any withdrawal to speak of, and my internist says I'm perfectly healthy. So I don't see how anyone could consider me an alcoholic."

"How would you describe yourself, Nell?"

"As an overdrinker," she replied. "An occasional overdrinker. An occasional, stress-related, problem overdrinker. But not an alcoholic."

Nell remained abstinent with the assistance of therapy and daily doses of disulfiram, a drug which she knew would make her violently ill if she drank. After about three months of treatment, her husband took her out to an expensive restaurant to show his appreciation for the effort she was making.

"I just want you to know how much I love you," he told her. "The kids are happy, and so am I."

"If you're happy, I'm happy," Nell said. "But do I really have to keep seeing the doctor? I really don't see why it's necessary, and I don't think it's helping me at all."

Her husband didn't like this turn in the conversation. "Aren't you afraid you'd drink again?"

"Not at all. I can keep taking the medication, silly. How could I drink again if I continue using that?"

Nell stopped seeing the therapist. A month afterward, her husband returned home late one night from a business trip to find her unconscious, drunk, on the couch.

Cognitive Error: Nell fails to complete the most important task of treatment: recognition of the illness. Her abstinence, though commendable, is entirely motivated by the desire to please her husband. When he expresses his pleasure, she takes that as a sign that everything is back to normal and she need not continue in treatment. Once she terminates therapy, it is only a matter of time until she stops taking the disulfiram and returns to drinking.

Alcoholics frequently give up alcohol not with the intention of treating their disease but simply to prove a point or defuse a specific crisis. As noted in Chapter 3, such motivation is by its very nature transient. When it disappears, abstinence will disappear as well.

To avoid this error: With the assistance of a counselor or other knowledgeable person, do a formal self-diagnosis exercise. Write out the history of your involvement with alcohol and other drugs, from the first contact to the present day. Use the appropriate Bell Charts (see Appendix 1) as your guide. Determine the stage of your addiction by noting where your most advanced symptom falls on the curve.

Then write in your own words a detailed description of what you believe is causing the problems in your life. If you do not believe you suffer from alcoholism or drug dependence, explain precisely why you feel that way, in writing. Discuss this with your counselor. Get his or her feedback.

Experiments with Control

Some addicts are quite capable of acknowledging their addiction while continuing to deny the need for ongoing abstinence. It's a form of *specific denial* that leads directly to relapse.

Case Illustration: Benny, age forty-two, had been treated four times for heroin addiction. In each case, he relapsed within a few days of his discharge from the hospital. Placed by the courts on methadone maintenance, Benny was quickly terminated from the program for use of cocaine and other drugs.

"Benny," the counselor said as he was admitted for yet another detoxification, "you say you're an addict. I've heard you get up and tell your story in group, and man, you are beautiful. You bring tears to my eyes. And yet, you yourself can't seem to get a week drug-free. Even on methadone. What is wrong here?"

"I dunno," Benny replied, embarrassed. "I've tried everything, and I just can't seem to stay away from junk. I'll be doing great, and something will happen, and I'll hit the skids."

"But Ben, you say you're doing great, but you're still using drugs. You've never turned in a clean urine test in your life."

"No, but I mean I'm working and everything, I got money coming in, I'm living the straight life. Then something happens and I'm back in here again."

"Wait a minute. You sound like you think it's okay to use drugs as long as you go to work and pay your bills."

"Well, sure. What's wrong with it? So I have a couple hits in the evening—I'm not out robbing nobody, or bein' a menace to society, am I? I'm a productive citizen. I just happen to live in a country where people think it's wrong to get high."

Cognitive Error: Though Ben readily identifies himself as an addict, he doesn't see the importance of abstinence because he doesn't see anything particularly wrong with addiction. In Ben's mind, the problem isn't addiction itself but the behavior associated with it. He strives not toward sobriety, but toward his vision of "successful" drug use.

To avoid this error: Make a list of all the health related consequences (both physical and psychological) that accompany addiction to alcohol and drugs. Use the books in the Suggested Reading List (see Appendix) to identify what these are. Discuss with a counselor or other knowledgeable person the adverse impact of alcohol and drugs on health. What evidence of that impact already exists in your history? What negative consequences could occur in the future?

Succumbing to Stress

Many alcoholics accumulate problems until they reach a point where one becomes the "straw that broke the camel's back," and justifies (in the addict's mind) the use of alcohol or drugs.

Case Illustration: Rudy, age thirty-two, president of his own successful interior design firm, had a long history of cocaine, alcohol, and sedative abuse. He was also treated three times in inpatient programs, remaining sober no more than six weeks following discharge.

"I do fine for a while, but you could say the pressure is building up even then," he told his therapist. "I can't pinpoint any one thing, but it just seems like I'm always worried about something. One of my friends will get sick (AIDS), and I'll start worrying about whether or not I'm HIV positive. Or a customer will make some unthinking remark, something homophobic, and I won't say anything but I'll be so upset I can't sleep for two or three nights. Or I'll have a fight with Brad, and the house will be like a demilitarized zone for a few days—and before I know it, I'm craving coke."

Cognitive Error: This one is fairly easy to identify. Rudy is not only experiencing tension, anxiety, and resentment—the basic components of a stress reaction—he's *accumulating* them. To each new crisis, Rudy brings the undischarged stress from the previous day's adversarial situation. He keeps his nervous system in a state of constant uproar, then wonders why it won't allow him to relax.

Rudy should learn to view himself not only as an addict but as a "stress junkie"—someone who can't let go of problems, and therefore is unable to achieve any level of serenity. Fortunately, this is treatable.

To avoid this error: Complete the following brief "stress accumulation inventory." Discuss the results with a counselor or other knowledgeable person, and make a plan for altering your responses. Read something by Albert Ellis on the Rational Emotive Therapy approach to stress reduction. Write "T" or "F" (true or false) after each of the following:

SECTION A:

1. I consider myself a perfectionist.
2. Other people tell me I am excessively critical.

SECTION B:

3. I believe that I have been badly treated by people in the past.
4. I often permit myself to be victimized or taken advantage of.

SECTION C:

5. I hate being made to wait for something.
6. I am often frustrated.

SECTION D:

7. I don't trust people easily.
8. I believe that the only person you can rely on is yourself.

SECTION E:

9. I don't like groups.
10. I consider myself a loner.

Now, total your scores for each of the five sections. Wherever you responded "true" to both questions in a section, read the relevant passage below.

SECTION A: PERFECTIONISM

Much of the stress you experience will stem from your tendency to demand too much from yourself and others. Remember: Because there is no perfection in our world, a perfectionist by definition is *never* satisfied.

SECTION B: RESENTMENT

For you, stress often results from lingering depression or anger about things that happened in the past, and from your feeling that other people are somehow manipulating or victimizing you. You sometimes break off or halt relationships because you feel someone is taking advantage of you.

SECTION C: LOW FRUSTRATION TOLERANCE

Stress for you occurs whenever you are made to wait for something, or cannot see the clear positive outcome of a situation. You want to control events so that things happen on schedule, and to your satisfaction. This is often linked to perfectionism.

SECTION D: MISTRUST

You sometimes experience stress in relationships because you have little faith that others have your interests at heart. You tend to make friends slowly and to guard against possible disappointment. When someone lets you down, you normally resolve never to allow this to happen again—which promotes isolation.

SECTION E: ISOLATION

Stress for you often stems simply from the company of strangers. You avoid situations where this occurs in favor of individual encounters or small, familiar groups. For you, treatment itself can be a source of stress, if it involves attendance at a group. Yet you often do best if you strive to overcome this anxiety, rather than giving in to it.

Becoming Complacent

When you stop drinking and doing drugs, your life normally improves. You stop getting in fights with the people around you, or getting arrested, or forgetting to pay your bills for months on end. Above all, you start to feel better physically and psychologically.

But even as you benefit from sobriety, you discover that it is more difficult to recall the pain of addiction. As that occurs, you may also forget the many reasons for remaining sober.

Case Illustration: Ben, a twenty-nine-year-old hod carrier, has had four outpatient treatments since age twenty-one. He's also been arrested six times for drunk driving, in four different states. He has attended Alcoholics Anonymous for the past six years, likes meetings, and has three sponsors. His longest period of continuous sobriety, however, is seven months. Following a slip, Ben attends meetings daily for a while, then begins to slack off, and eventually stops attending altogether. He says drinking begins shortly afterward, though one of his sponsors, believes he quits going to meetings because he is already drinking secretly. Ben denies any problems "other than the ones everybody has—sex and money. You know, not enough of either."

Ben and his wife argue a great deal. She claims he is a compulsive liar and gambler who doesn't care about anyone but himself. He says; "I probably deserve that—I put her through a lot." She wants him to enter therapy for lying and gambling. He resists: "My problem is I stop going to meetings. Other things come up, and I let them get in the way. Besides, when I'm sober I feel like I don't *need* anybody's help. I start thinking that I can't keep going to meetings all my life—I have to grow up sometimes."

Cognitive Error: Actually, Ben understands the problem perfectly. He just doesn't do anything about it. As soon as Ben recuperates from his previous slip, he begins psychologically preparing himself for the next one. He resents having to attend meetings because he doesn't connect attendance with his sobriety. It isn't long before he reintroduces alcohol.

Note how Ben's wife misinterprets the importance of his behavior because she views it through a *psychogenic* model (see Chapter 3). When Ben is drinking heavily, he has a tendency to gamble as well as to get caught in meaningless, transparent falsehoods. She interprets this as proof positive that he is in fact a compulsive gambler and a pathological liar. Accordingly, she minimizes the importance of Ben's alcoholism in favor of an effort to engage him in therapy for these other disorders, which she concludes are responsible for his relapses. That's typical of psychogenic reasoning—the alcoholic drinks because of some underlying psychological or personality problem, and cannot remain sober unless and until this problem is identified and addressed.

The flaw in such reasoning becomes obvious when we realize that Ben doesn't drink because he gambles and tells lies—he gambles and tells lies when he's drinking. In fact, we have no evidence at all that gambling even occurs without the trigger of alcohol consumption. Perhaps if Ben establishes more than a few consecutive months of sobriety, these problem behaviors will disappear completely. Even if they don't, any therapist will find them easier to treat if Ben is sober rather than drunk.

To avoid this error: No matter how well you're feeling or doing, continue to attend meetings for a year. Where possible, assist newcomers in establishing their own sobriety.

Concurrent Medical Problems

Alcoholics frequently suffer from other medical disorders as well: diabetes, coronary heart disease, hypertension, cancer, emphysema, arthritis, orthopedic conditions, and so forth. Sometimes these are the direct or indirect result of alcohol and drugs; sometimes they are largely unrelated. In either case, medical problems can undermine sobriety.

Case Illustration: Dina, thirty-nine, is a school psychologist with a history of addiction to alcohol, sedatives, and prescription painkillers, for which she has been in treatment for more than three years. She is also receiving treatment for a variety of chronic medical problems which sometimes precipitate episodes of such severity that she must seek help at the local emergency room. Following these visits she is normally given a supply of painkillers and muscle relaxants which results in a relapse. Within a few weeks, she is stumbling and falling around the house, or passing into unconsciousness because of an overdose. Her husband has filed for divorce.

"I don't want to take drugs," she insists, "but I am not about to endure that kind of pain if I can avoid it."

"But the doctors say the pain is chronic, Dina—they say the drugs don't really help, and you could learn to live without them," says her sister.

"They don't know how I feel. No one could tolerate the pain I have to put up with."

Cognitive Error: Though Dina spends most of her waking hours in treatment for one medical condition or another, she really doesn't cooperate with her physicians at all. They see the futility of trying to treat such nebulous chronic complaints with addictive medications, and strongly encourage her to seek alternative methods for pain control. But Dina stubbornly insists that her pain is worse than anyone else's pain, and therefore justifies relapse, despite the problems it causes everywhere else in her life.

To avoid this error: Learn about nonaddictive alternatives for relief of chronic pain. Contact your local Chronic Pain clinic and investigate a support group for pain sufferers.

Concurrent Psychiatric Problems

Sometimes the second condition complicating recovery is an untreated psychiatric disorder, such as chronic depression, bipolar syndrome, or an anxiety disorder.

Case Illustration: Dwayne, thirty-six, began experiencing dramatic swings in mood and behavior after only a few weeks away from alcohol and cocaine. By the fourth month of sobriety, he was cycling between disabling, week-long episodes of depression and shorter bursts of hyperactive, near manic behavior. His boss at the tire company insisted he be evaluated by a psychiatrist.

"I think you're bipolar, Dwayne," the psychiatrist told him. "I'd like to put you on lithium, to level out some of those extremes of mood."

"No way, Doc. It took me six years to get off drugs, and I'm not taking anything stronger than an aspirin. I'm through with chemicals."

Three months later, Dwayne was back in the psychiatrist's office. Two weeks earlier he had gotten drunk and gone on a furniture buying spree, spending $11,000 decorating a house he did not own. "It made sense at the time. I was planning on buying the house. But when the loan fell through—I realized how crazy the whole thing was. And then I got really depressed. I was actually thinking about killing myself."

"Lithium, Dwayne," the doctor said.

"How about I just come in once a week and we talk about it? Then if I run into trouble, maybe we'll do the medication."

Ninety days afterward, Dwayne was admitted to detox following an abortive suicide attempt. He finally consented to the use of medication and was able to remain abstinent from that point.

Cognitive Error: Dwayne responds to his psychiatric condition with the same defensive and stubborn attitude which kept him away from addiction treatment for so long. He is wary of authority, and thinks he can help himself better than any doctor can (this skepticism might seem very familiar to you). He mistakenly assumes that it is possible to remain sober in the face of florid psychiatric problems.

To avoid this error: If symptoms of depression, mania, or other such psychiatric disorders persist, seek evaluation by a psychiatrist or psychologist who specializes in treating the chemically dependent. You can often find them associated with the nearest treatment program. Discuss the symptoms with them, and listen to their assessment.

Complications of Recovery

Not infrequently, some symptom of alcohol or drug toxicity—insomnia, sexual dysfunction, fluctuations in energy level—persists well into recovery. This often triggers an overreaction on the part of the addict, which can lead to relapse.

Case Illustration: Miranda, age twenty-one, has been unable to sleep a full night since quitting drugs. She goes to sleep easily enough but wakes up nearly every hour and usually cannot get back to sleep after four AM. She complains bitterly about this to her doctor.

"I can't be expected to study or pass courses if I can't get a decent night's sleep. I never had this problem when I was using."

"You're healthy, Miranda," the doctor replies. "You sleep most of the night. This is probably just temporary. Your body will adjust."

"A lot you know," she says. "Look, can't you give me something to help me sleep?"

"You've been addicted to everything in the Physician's Desk Reference. I'd be afraid to medicate you. Besides, even in the best of circumstances, sleeping pills are only a short-term remedy. For somebody like you, they're worse than not sleeping."

Miranda pretended to comply but secretly began shopping for a doctor who would prescribe a sleeping medication for her. She finally found one in an unsuspecting gynecologist. The pills worked well for about a week, then seemed to lose their effectiveness. Miranda was faced with a choice: either suffer insomnia, or increase the dose. She chose the latter.

Two months later, she was admitted to the hospital in a coma, induced by an overdose of sleeping pills in combination with alcohol.

Cognitive Error: Miranda assumes that a persistent symptom is a *permanent* problem, in spite of the doctor's assurance to the contrary.

To avoid this error: If you're troubled by a problem which might simply be an outgrowth of slow healing—insomnia, sexual dysfunction, etc.—seek evaluation by a specialist who is also familiar with the process of recovery. Consult your local treatment center for a referral. Describe your symptoms to them, and listen to the advice they give. If they advise you to be patient, then strive to do just that. If they advise undertaking a course of treatment for a related problem, then follow that direction. Exercise a reasonable measure of faith in their expertise.

Family Dysfunction

Sometimes the same people who fervently support the attempt at recovery can unwittingly provoke a relapse.

Case Illustration: Vanda, a thirty-seven-year-old physician, was suspended from practice for misuse of prescription drugs and forced to live with her parents following treatment for addiction. She quickly fell into a pattern of complaining to her therapist about her parents' behavior.

"The day I arrived, they searched my bags," she said. "They tried to do it secretly, but I could tell. Every time I walk past my mother, she sniffs the air to see if she can smell alcohol. Very subtle. They insist I go to church with them on Sundays—I told them I'm an atheist, but they pay no attention. They're even bringing men over to the house to meet me. Prospective suitors, I suppose."

The therapist looked puzzled. "I thought you were a lesbian."

"So did I," Vanda replied. "I guess they figure that as long as they've got me under their control, they might as well fix that, too."

"Well," the therapist said, "They're pretty old. Maybe you could just sort of ignore it. You'll be gone in a couple of months."

"Easier said than done. Sometimes I want to throttle them. I don't think I can take much more of it."

"Vanda, what choice do you have? You're massively in debt. You've got to stay in this area for treatment. It was nice of them even to take you in. Seems to me you're just going to have to stay sober, grin, and bear it."

As much as she tried, Vanda felt herself losing control of her anger. After one particularly tense argument over her resistance to attending a church social, Vanda stormed out of the house and went for a drive. Three hours later she stopped at a late-night tavern in a neighboring state and drank three double vodkas and a quart of beer. She became so loud and aggressive the bartender threw her out.

Vanda began the long drive home with a six-pack of beer in the seat beside her. She was arrested for drunk driving thirty miles from the bar.

Cognitive Error: Vanda uses the tension with her parents as an excuse to return to alcohol. Of course, drinking doesn't solve her problem; it exacerbates it. Not only does she collect a DWI arrest—which as her third such offense resulted in a year's suspension of her driver's license and approximately $3000 in legal fees—but her behavior reinforced her parents' stereotypical concept of alcoholism. The situation might well have been relieved had the therapist involved Vanda's parents in a family counseling and education program. After all, their approach simply reflected the narrow, moralistic view of addiction popular in their generation. Viewing their daughter's problems through the prism of psychogenic thinking, they were trying to cure her by bringing her back to God, acting as watchdogs against possible relapse, and introducing her to potential husbands. By their lights, they were expressing their love for her.

To avoid this error: Encourage your loved ones and concerned persons to involve themselves in family education or counseling.

Consult the Suggested Reading List in the Appendix for appropriate reading. Support the idea of attending Alanon or another
family-oriented support group. Don't take the position that it's none
of their business. It is, whether that pleases you or not. After all,
Vanda's parents' religious beliefs were no more than a temporary
imposition—one she could easily have ignored.

High-Risk Environment

Many alcoholics attempt to stay sober while surrounding themselves with "slippery" places and people. This makes relapse not
only more likely, but actually convenient.

Case Illustration: Frank, age thirty, had been a bartender since his
college years. His own escalating drinking finally led him to seek
treatment in an outpatient program. After a few weeks of treatment, it became obvious to both Frank and his counselor that the
principle obstacle to success was going to be Frank's occupation.
Whenever he was around alcohol, he craved it constantly.

"I know people who have been sober for years and still tend bar,"
Frank told the counselor.

"Maybe so, Frank, but it's beginning to look like you aren't one of
them."

"Dammit, I'm a good bartender," he replied. "I like bars. I like the
people, I like the hours, I like the atmosphere. Christ, I've practically lived in bars since I was eighteen years old. Besides, they
don't allow you to drink while you're working. I'm probably safer
there than I am at home in my apartment. Why should I have to
change?"

"I don't know," the counselor said. "But I think you have to."

Frank remained sober for six months, attending Secular Sobriety
meetings, taking Antabuse, and seeing his counselor once weekly.
But the craving for alcohol never left, and even he described his
sobriety as "white-knuckle." Still, Frank believed that his success in
remaining alcohol-free was evidence that he had been right all
along. He was able to continue tending bar while practicing a program of recovery.

One night while Frank was closing up the bar, he began flirting with a very attractive younger woman who had pleaded with him for a final drink after last call. He mixed her the perfect martini: two olives, shaken not stirred, a breath of vermouth.

As she drank, she glanced up at him seductively. He thought she looked a little drunk.

"Do you have a girlfriend?" she asked.

"No," Frank lied, trying not to stare at her cleavage.

"Would you like one, temporarily?"

"Sure."

"Then mix us both another of these, and let's go to my place."

"Uh, I can't," he stammered. "I mean, I'll make you one, but I don't drink."

"Sure you don't," she said. "What are you, an alcoholic?"

"Actually, yes."

"Can't handle it, huh?"

"I can," Frank said, feeling suddenly defensive. "I choose not to." She laughed. "Sissy."

Angry, Frank mixed two martinis, passed one to her, and downed the second. As soon as the alcohol hit his brain, it was as though all the problems, the worries, the anxiety of the past months had been washed away. He felt like himself again.

He awoke the next morning to discover he was still behind the bar—or to be accurate, stretched out naked on top of it. The Korean cleaning lady was staring at him, mop in hand, an expression of complete puzzlement on her face. The alluring young woman of the night before was nowhere in sight.

Cognitive Error: Frank assumes that simple willpower will be enough to avoid the constant temptation to relapse that is inherent in his occupation. He ignores the warning signs of potential relapse, such as persistent craving and an uncomfortable sobriety.

To avoid this error: Make every effort to ensure that the initial weeks and months of abstinence are as *easy* to achieve as possible. Don't put yourself in high-risk situations and rely on your willpower to get you through. Later, after your sobriety is more firmly established, you can take some controlled risks. But now may not be the right time.

To sum up, understanding and preventing relapse is one area where the skepticism and realistic bent of the nonbeliever can be an asset. It's often said that when it comes to change, most of us are our own worst enemies—we permit ourselves to rationalize a return to the old ways of thinking and acting, even to our detriment. The toughmindedness which characterizes the nonbeliever can thus be turned to advantage. Just have the courage to look at the contradictions in your own behavior as critically as you examined the tenets of organized religion.

Recommended Reading

ALCOHOLICS ANONYMOUS, AA World Services, 1955.
The "Big Book" of AA. Read Chapter 5, "How It Works."

DON'T HELP by Ronald Rogers and Chandler McMillin, Bantam, 1989.
A guide to the treatment of alcoholism as a chronic disease, using Milam's approach as a basis. Note especially the difference between the *maintenance* and *loss of control* patterns and the discussion of "comparing out" in Chapter 4, "How Alcoholics Drink." Note also the description of mixing and matching various chemicals in Chapter 5, and of the various models of alcoholism in Chapter 2.

800-COCAINE, by Mark Gold, M.D., Bantam 1984.
If your primary drug was cocaine, take the self-test in Chapter 7. Wherever you answer "yes" to a given symptom, be sure to read the page reference for a fuller explanation.

HOW TO STAY SOBER, by James Christopher, Prometheus Books, 1988.
An introduction to recovery the Secular Sobriety way.

LIVING SOBER, 1975
Practical advice on the basics of recovery.

NARCOTICS ANONYMOUS, 1982.
The NA equivalent of the Big Book.

THE SMALL BOOK, Jack Trimpey, 1992.
A description of the RR philosophy and program.

TWELVE STEPS AND TWELVE TRADITIONS, AA World Services, 1953.
The traditional interpretation of the Steps and how they work.

THE TWELVE STEPS REVISITED, Ronald Rogers and Chandler McMillin, Bantam, 1989.
A reinterpretation of the Steps as a way to recover from a chronic disease.

UNDER THE INFLUENCE, James Milam and Katherine Ketcham, Bantam, 1986.
The single best introduction to chronic disease model of alcoholism. Pay special attention to Chapter 7, "The Alcoholic." As you read, make a list of italicized terms found in the discussion of early, middle, and late-stage alcoholism.

The Progression and Recovery of the Alcoholic in the Disease of Alcoholism

To be read from left to right.

ADAPTIVE STAGE

Drinks to feel better
Drinks to relax
Drinks to feel stimulated
Drinks for any reason
Frequency of drinking increases
Amount of drinking increases
Feels lucky to be able to drink without getting drunk
Nausea early in day
Mild shakes which "cure" themselves
Daily drinking
Night sweats
Drinks inappropriate amounts
Drinks at inappropriate times
Drinks in inappropriate places

Drinks with improved functioning
Mild irritability the "morning after"
Preoccupation with next drink
Gets drunk more frequently
Loss of other interests
Begins taking "the hair of the dog" or tranquilizers
Blames drinking on problems
May seek psychological help for problems

DEPENDENT STAGE

Drinks with other "sadder cases"
Is questioned by others about drinking
Suffers seizures or DT's
Work, family, personal problems increase
Severe physical penalty if drinking is stopped
Loss of appetite
Digestive problems
Heart racing
Bruises easily

Shakes increase
Efforts to quit fail
Blackouts
Thinking confused
Memory lapses
Increases in colds—flu's—infections
Notices swelling and puffiness
Numbness or tingling in arms, legs, feet
Blood in urine or stools
Pain in stomach or back
Broken blood vessels particularly in face
Yellow eyes or skin
Seeks medical help
Life becomes unpredictable
Loss of control over alcohol intake

DETERIORATIVE STAGE

Enters treatment because of physical illness or is coerced into treatment because of social-job-behavioral problems

Patient feels guilty, angry, depressed over his/her situation
Medical condition is treated
Patient is detoxified

RE-EDUCATION

Re-education begins
Learns alcoholism is a disease process
Denies alcoholism — compares out
Emotions are augmented
Compares experience with learning
Self-diagnosed with some minimization
Admits having the disease without reservations
Learns how to treat it
Begins to take personal responsibility by changing thinking and behavior
Makes commitment to treat illness
Anger, depression, guilt subside

Becomes hopeful
Helps fellow patients
Begins working in groups
Compares in at AA meetings

RECOVERY

Signs for aftercare
Not drinking becomes unconditional
Accepts oneself as a nondrinking alcoholic
Becomes willing to go to any lengths for sobriety
Maintains recovery program

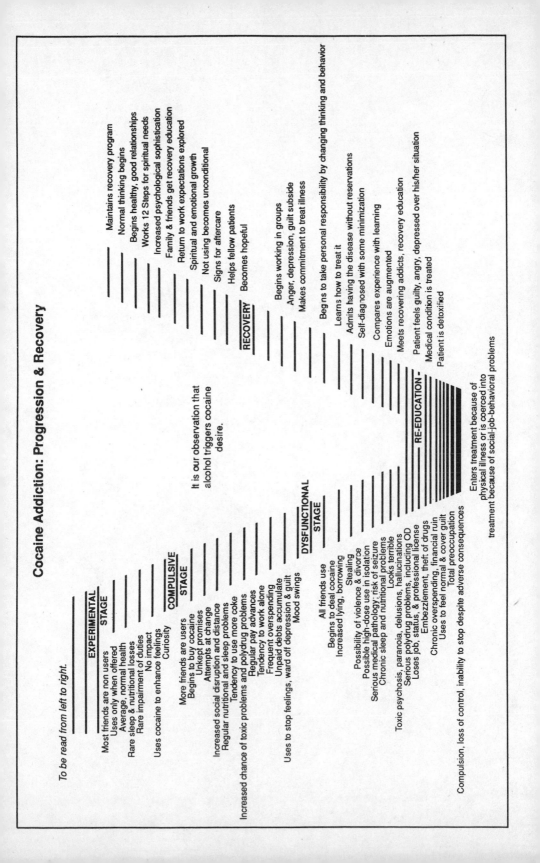

Cocaine Addiction: Progression & Recovery

To be read from left to right.

EXPERIMENTAL STAGE

Most friends are non users
Uses only when offered
Average, normal health
Rare sleep & nutritional losses
Rare impairment of duties
No impact
Uses cocaine to enhance feelings
Curiosity

COMPULSIVE STAGE

More friends are users
Begins to buy cocaine
Unkept promises
Attempts at change
Increased social disruption and distance
Regular nutritional and sleep problems
Tendency to use more coke
Increased chance of toxic problems and polydrug problems
Regular pay advances
Tendency to work alone
Frequent overspending
Unpaid debts accumulate
Uses to stop feelings, ward off depression & guilt
Mood swings

DYSFUNCTIONAL STAGE

All friends use
Begins to deal cocaine
Increased lying, borrowing
Stealing
Possibility of violence & divorce
Possible high-dose use in isolation
Serious medical pathology; risk of seizure
Chronic sleep and nutritional problems
Looks terrible
Toxic psychosis, paranoia, delusions, hallucinations
Serious polydrug problems, including OD
Loses job, status, & professional license
Embezzlement, theft, of drugs
Chronic overspending, financial ruin
Uses to feel normal & cover guilt
Total preoccupation
Compulsion, loss of control, inability to stop despite adverse consequences

It is our observation that alcohol triggers cocaine desire.

RE-EDUCATION –

Enters treatment because of physical illness or is coerced into treatment because of social-job-behavioral problems
Patient is detoxified
Medical condition is treated
Patient feels guilty, angry, depressed over his/her situation
Meets recovering addicts, recovery education
Emotions are augmented
Compares experience with learning
Self-diagnosed with some minimization
Admits having the disease without reservations
Learns how to treat it
Begins to take personal responsibility by changing thinking and behavior

RECOVERY

Makes commitment to treat illness
Anger, depression, guilt subside
Begins working in groups
Becomes hopeful
Helps fellow patients
Signs for aftercare
Not using becomes unconditional
Spiritual and emotional growth
Return to work expectations explored
Family & friends get recovery education
Increased psychological sophistication
Works 12 Steps for spiritual needs
Begins healthy, good relationships
Normal thinking begins
Maintains recovery program

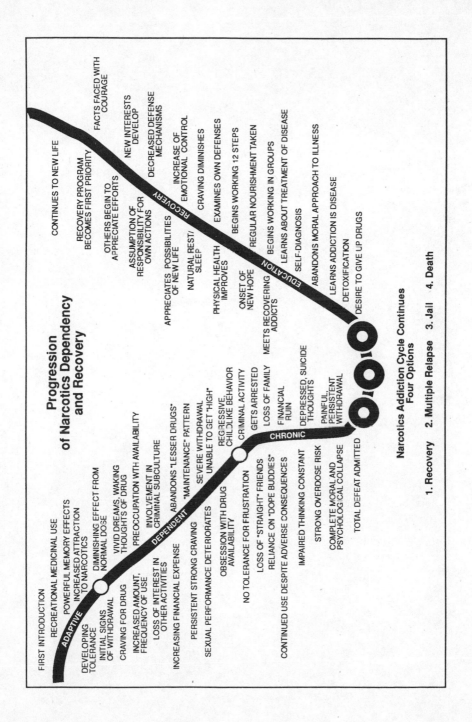

Progression
of Narcotics Dependency
and Recovery

ADAPTIVE

FIRST INTRODUCTION
RECREATIONAL MEDICINAL USE
POWERFUL MEMORY EFFECTS
INCREASED ATTRACTION TO NARCOTICS
DEVELOPING TOLERANCE
DIMINISHING EFFECT FROM NORMAL DOSE
INITIAL SIGNS OF WITHDRAWAL
VIVID DREAMS, WAKING THOUGHTS OF DRUG
CRAVING FOR DRUG
PREOCCUPATION WITH AVAILABILITY

DEPENDENT

INCREASED AMOUNT, FREQUENCY OF USE
INVOLVEMENT IN CRIMINAL SUBCULTURE
LOSS OF INTEREST IN OTHER ACTIVITIES
ABANDONS "LESSER DRUGS"
INCREASING FINANCIAL EXPENSE
"MAINTENANCE" PATTERN
PERSISTENT STRONG CRAVING
SEVERE WITHDRAWAL
UNABLE TO GET "HIGH"
SEXUAL PERFORMANCE DETERIORATES
REGRESSIVE, CHILDLIKE BEHAVIOR
OBSESSION WITH DRUG AVAILABILITY
CRIMINAL ACTIVITY

CHRONIC

NO TOLERANCE FOR FRUSTRATION
GETS ARRESTED
LOSS OF "STRAIGHT" FRIENDS
LOSS OF FAMILY
RELIANCE ON "DOPE BUDDIES"
FINANCIAL RUIN
CONTINUED USE DESPITE ADVERSE CONSEQUENCES
DEPRESSED, SUICIDE THOUGHTS
IMPAIRED THINKING CONSTANT
PAINFUL, PERSISTENT WITHDRAWAL
STRONG OVERDOSE RISK
COMPLETE MORAL AND PSYCHOLOGICAL COLLAPSE
TOTAL DEFEAT ADMITTED

Narcotics Addiction Cycle Continues
Four Options

1. Recovery   2. Multiple Relapse   3. Jail   4. Death

EDUCATION

DESIRE TO GIVE UP DRUGS
DETOXIFICATION
LEARNS ADDICTION IS DISEASE
ABANDONS MORAL APPROACH TO ILLNESS
SELF-DIAGNOSIS
LEARNS ABOUT TREATMENT OF DISEASE
BEGINS WORKING IN GROUPS
REGULAR NOURISHMENT TAKEN
MEETS RECOVERING ADDICTS
ONSET OF NEW HOPE
PHYSICAL HEALTH IMPROVES
BEGINS WORKING 12 STEPS
NATURAL REST/ SLEEP
EXAMINES OWN DEFENSES

RECOVERY

APPRECIATES POSSIBILITIES OF NEW LIFE
CRAVING DIMINISHES
INCREASE OF EMOTIONAL CONTROL
ASSUMPTION OF RESPONSIBILITY FOR OWN ACTIONS
DECREASED DEFENSE MECHANISMS
OTHERS BEGIN TO APPRECIATE EFFORTS
NEW INTERESTS DEVELOP
RECOVERY PROGRAM BECOMES FIRST PRIORITY
FACTS FACED WITH COURAGE
CONTINUES TO NEW LIFE

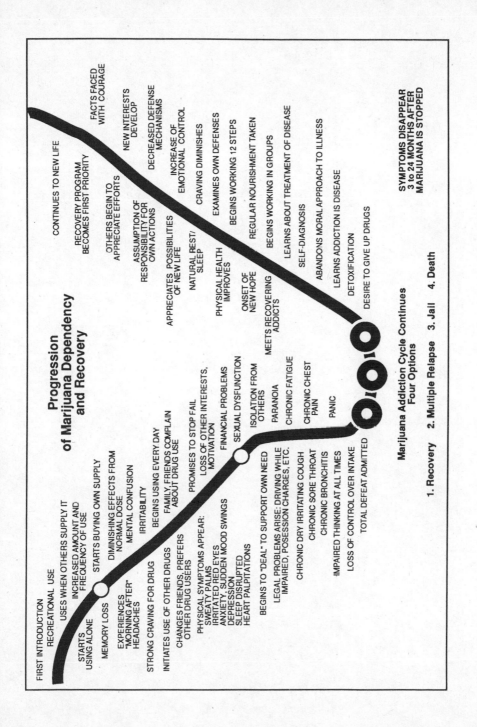

Progression
of Marijuana Dependency
and Recovery

FIRST INTRODUCTION
RECREATIONAL USE
USES WHEN OTHERS SUPPLY IT
INCREASED AMOUNT AND
FREQUENCY OF USE
STARTS
USING ALONE
STARTS BUYING OWN SUPPLY
MEMORY LOSS
DIMINISHING EFFECTS FROM
NORMAL DOSE
EXPERIENCES
"MORNING AFTER"
HEADACHES
MENTAL CONFUSION
IRRITABILITY
STRONG CRAVING FOR DRUG
BEGINS USING EVERY DAY
INITIATES USE OF OTHER DRUGS
FAMILY, FRIENDS COMPLAIN
ABOUT DRUG USE
CHANGES FRIENDS, PREFERS
OTHER DRUG USERS
PROMISES TO STOP FAIL
PHYSICAL SYMPTOMS APPEAR:
SWEATY PALMS
LOSS OF OTHER INTERESTS,
MOTIVATION
IRRITATED RED EYES
ANXIETY, SUDDEN MOOD SWINGS
FINANCIAL PROBLEMS
DEPRESSION
SLEEP DISRUPTED
SEXUAL DYSFUNCTION
HEART PALPITATIONS
ISOLATION FROM
OTHERS
BEGINS TO "DEAL" TO SUPPORT OWN NEED
PARANOIA
LEGAL PROBLEMS ARISE: DRIVING WHILE
IMPAIRED, POSESSION CHARGES, ETC.
CHRONIC FATIGUE
CHRONIC DRY IRRITATING COUGH
CHRONIC CHEST
PAIN
CHRONIC SORE THROAT
CHRONIC BRONCHITIS
PANIC
IMPAIRED THINKING AT ALL TIMES
LOSS OF CONTROL OVER INTAKE
TOTAL DEFEAT ADMITTED

CONTINUES TO NEW LIFE
FACTS FACED
WITH COURAGE
RECOVERY PROGRAM
BECOMES FIRST PRIORITY
NEW INTERESTS
DEVELOP
OTHERS BEGIN TO
APPRECIATE EFFORTS
DECREASED DEFENSE
MECHANISMS
ASSUMPTION OF
RESPONSIBILITY FOR
OWN ACTIONS
INCREASE OF
EMOTIONAL CONTROL
APPRECIATES POSSIBILITIES
OF NEW LIFE
CRAVING DIMINISHES
NATURAL REST/
SLEEP
EXAMINES OWN DEFENSES
PHYSICAL HEALTH
IMPROVES
BEGINS WORKING 12 STEPS
ONSET OF
NEW HOPE
REGULAR NOURISHMENT TAKEN
MEETS RECOVERING
ADDICTS
BEGINS WORKING IN GROUPS
LEARNS ABOUT TREATMENT OF DISEASE
SELF-DIAGNOSIS
ABANDONS MORAL APPROACH TO ILLNESS
LEARNS ADDICTION IS DISEASE
DETOXIFICATION
DESIRE TO GIVE UP DRUGS

SYMPTOMS DISAPPEAR
3 to 24 MONTHS AFTER
MARIJUANA IS STOPPED

Marijuana Addiction Cycle Continues
Four Options

1. Recovery   2. Multiple Relapse   3. Jail   4. Death

Index

Other Perigee Titles of Interest